By

Aaron Robbins

Table of Contents

Dedication

For my family. We supported each other and came together through a most difficult time.

For Rosemary. You were our champion.

Acknowledgment

Dr. Abayomi Ajayi and his team at Brantford Gerneral Hospital

Hamilton General Hospital, Department of Cardiology.

My Mom, Leila Mason, who consistently encouraged, and supported the writing of my story to help others.

About the Author

Aaron Robbins grew up in Markham, Ontario, Canada. After fine art studies at York University in Toronto, he married and moved to the west coast of British Columbia. In the Pacific North West, Aaron pursued his love of mountain biking by founding a successful race team, competing in Provincial and National Cup races. He continued his art and established representation in fine art galleries. His paintings were placed in collections in Canada, the United States and Europe. Aaron co-founded the Burrard Inlet Artists Association and the Electronic Avenue Art Gallery.

In 2007, Aaron and his young family moved back to Ontario where he is now working in real estate and continues with his painting. After Aaron's NDE, he has a much closer relationship with God and shares his story to those willing and needing to hear about the reality of our eternal soul. He wishes to bring healing comfort to those seeking to know what happens after we depart this earthly dimension.

Prologue

After racing for five hours around the mountains of eastern Squamish—halfway between Vancouver and the slopes of Whistler—we packed up the cycling team tent, table, chairs, banners, and promotional materials and said our goodbyes to the remaining team members. Along the drive home on the coastal highway, forested mountains rose up to our left and right, a sheer drop down to the dark blue ocean. Louise, without hesitation, drove home after the races. My legs were stiff and sore, and my mind was somewhere else. After driving just a few minutes, the hum of the tires traveling the paved roads usually caused Olivia to fall asleep in her seat. After a long day of being outdoors, running around to viewing areas, sometimes working the feed zones, and being my personal cheering squad, exhaustion set in. The ride home was quiet as I looked out the window, contemplating my performance, my physical condition, my aches and pains, my recovery, and how I was going to be able to perform at work the next day.

That day, racing in Squamish, I had finished the 67-kilometer (about 41 miles) race with a time of 5 hours and 17 minutes, placing me in the top 400 of 800 riders. I had a strong and dedicated team of athletes. One of my racers placed on the podium that day and then proceeded to ride his bike the 64 kilometers (about 37 miles) back to Vancouver. I, on the other hand, was the slowest of the race team but was cut some slack as I was also the founder, owner, and general manager of the team. At 5'11," I was 162 pounds of lean muscle.

I rode my mountain bike at least 8 hours a week on a diverse mix of terrain, hiked on the weekends with my family, ate healthy, and ultimately lived a clean and active life. It didn't seem to matter how much I trained or how much I thought I was in great shape; I seemed to be towards the back end of every race. My stamina was present, and I finished very long and demanding races, but the intensity and physical conviction for speed were hard to sustain. On the drives back from the races, I would mentally beat myself up, not knowing why I was not able to perform with the same intensity as my peers. I kept going over and over how I could change my training, get more riding time, take better supplements, eat better, ride a lighter bike, and use better tires…my thoughts were always in a vicious circle without coming to any definite conclusion as to my lack of performance. It took another fourteen years to finally realize and understand why nothing seemed to be working, and I'm surprised I didn't die in those same mountains I loved.

Then, my dad passed away in 2017. He was the spiritual head of our family, having devoted most of his life to God's work within his business practices and missionary work. Until his passing, much of my spiritual life was lived vicariously through his testimonies. Any testament of my faith involved experiences with my dad and stories he told, preached, and wrote about. A few months had passed since his death, and I went into conversational prayer while driving to work one sunny afternoon.

"Heavenly Father, my dad is with you now, and my whole life, I have lived under his spiritual umbrella. I have used his stories, his teachings, and his testimonials to talk about You. Heavenly Father, I need my own story, my own testimony to relay to others and to talk about You. I need a testimony that is close to me and personal so I can relay the experience with passion and understanding."

Feeling satisfied with my prayer and happy with myself for taking the initiative to step up and fill my dad's shoes, I continued on my drive to work. The long days of summer passed one by one, and daily life resumed, not knowing that God had listened, heard my prayer, and was setting the stage to answer my prayer in the biggest and most unexpected way possible…

All I have to say about that car ride and prayer that day is to *be careful what you pray for.*

Beginning on Monday, the First Mouthful of Salt Water

The afternoon is hot, and the sun is at its peak for the day as I draw deep breaths inward through my mouth, attempting to fill my lungs with as much oxygen as possible. My arms are spread wide across the handlebars to open my chest so my lungs are not constricted and can expand to their fullest. I need as much oxygen as possible to feed my tired muscles and keep myself moving forward. My heart rate is really high, and at this point, the volume of oxygen I need is past the physical capabilities of my nose. I can't last like this for much longer. I must get my breathing and heart rate under control. Sweat is covering my entire body, and I feel the drips cascading down my face. At the end of my nose, the sweat collects into a small tear-shaped pool before it drips to the dusty ground. I force myself to breathe in through my nose and exhale out my mouth to lower my heart rate and settle my body. My core is working hard, transferring as much energy as it can to my hips and legs to keep pushing the peddles forward. I slide my thumb and forefinger to the rapid-fire trigger shifters on my mountain bike, and after a few gear changes, I'm able to find the right gears to optimize the expenditure on my muscles with the most forward movement possible. I am over halfway through the infamous Test of Metal race.

"Dad, Dad!"

I hear my daughter's voice as I snap out of my daydreaming.

"Daddy!!"

Opening my eyes to see a seat right in front of me, my tray is upright, and the plane is full of people. My arm slightly presses against the stranger next to me, who is also taking a few minutes rest with his head bobbing to the side and mouth slightly open.

"Dad, look out the window!" said my youngest daughter, Lily, with excitement in her voice from across the aisle. She is sitting beside her big sister, Olivia, pointing towards her small oval window.

Through the window, I can see the shores of the Continental United States slowly disappearing behind us and the edge of the Caribbean Sea with its turquoise blue waters. The nose of the plane begins to shift slightly downward, and pressure in the cabin increases. Within a few minutes, little islands with patches of green foliage surrounded by white sand and the vast sea come into view. Our descent towards the tropical, sandy beaches of Cuba has begun. It is the start of a weeklong getaway from the cold, ice, and snow of our Canadian hometown.

It was February thirteenth, and 2 a.m. came early, especially after a night of anticipation and anxiousness concerning our week to come. The lights slowly came on throughout our house. From the windows of our small brick bungalow, the light didn't push far into the night, as it was pitch-black outside. The house was unusually quiet as we all shuffled around, getting last-minute things and lining up for the single sink in the bathroom. The bathroom door opened and closed so many times it was hard to find the right moment to sneak in between my eleven and seventeen-year-old daughters. I'm sure Olivia and Lily's sleep that night was not great, as the excitement of the trip was building for days ahead of departure. For weeks, Lily and I would visit the Cuban resort's website. The reviews and photos of the white sandy beach, the multiple pools with a small waterfall, a swim up bar, and plentiful food, all seemed like a dream.

This trip was to be a new, exciting, and educational trip for them, seeing another culture and demographic. I had travelled when I was younger, but not extensively. I took two trips to the Caribbean, and one was to the island of Haiti. It was a beautiful country with beautiful people, but seeing the poverty and living conditions so unlike what I was used to made a big impact on me. Although I came from a divorced family, with a single mom who was young and struggling; comparatively, our North American society was a luxury. After seeing the shanty towns with steel-roofed shacks, swollen belly children bathing in the roadside ditches, and evidence of leprosy, I felt much more grateful for what my brother and I had. I wanted this trip to have a similar impact on my children. I wanted them to see a culture of need rather than want. I wanted them to see the beautiful resilience of a people and culture.

The bitter cold of winter lingered in Southern Ontario. It was -10 Celsius. Opening the door of our home to transfer our luggage to our van, we were met by the sharp bite of the cold on our faces and crunchy snow and ice beneath our feet. The sky above was overcast and grey, but the wind was quiet, and it wasn't snowing.

My wife, Louise, was not going on this trip with us. The vacation was to be a father—daughter trip. Louise didn't like the idea of roasting her fair skin on a beach. Our dog needed someone to look after her, and Louise was looking forward to having time at home to herself, something she very rarely had since we had our children.

We threw our luggage into the back and all got into our van with the defroster blasting heat to keep the windshield clear from ice. Louise was driving. She is truly a morning person and the most awake of all of us. She had also traveled through different parts of Europe and Japan eight times in the last couple of years for work, so, she knew the best way to the airport, where to go once we got there, and approximately how long it would take. I looked back towards the rear seats to see two very excited and slightly nervous girls. With the sound of cracking ice and snow under our tires, we left our driveway and drove through the early hours of the morning towards the airport.

Driving to the airport, peering out the window at the dull, grey winter landscape of snow-covered barren farm fields and darkened rural homes, I felt a heaviness of responsibility. The pressure of being the only parent and caregiver so far away and out of reach from Louise was unfamiliar to me. My "dad" persona is on the lesser side of seriousness, creating fantasy and adventures in almost everything we do. Louise, on the other hand, was the supermom who always had things organized, scheduled, and prepared. I felt insecure about taking on this weeklong trip and being the only parent. I rationalized, *I have to make this trip as fun as possible.* But I wanted to be there as someone who had traveled before, and I could rely on the natural order of things. I had to reason with myself, *what could go wrong.* We were taking a direct flight and landing at an airport that services the local resorts. The resort was only about 25 to 30 minutes from the airport in the area of Cayo Coco, which existed for the resorts and tourism. Food was provided, so I didn't have to search out good restaurants and find accommodating meals for the family. The activities were taken care of, and entertainment was taken care of…I was set! I was able to relax as we met our important deadline of getting to the flight, *it was all good*!

We were hit with the beautiful warmth of the tropical sun as we stepped out of the plane onto the loading ramp leading to the tarmac. A slight breeze and blue skies seemed to bid us welcome. The airport guide directed us to the terminal of Jardines Del Rey airport, a large two-story white with blue trim terminal building.

With Carry-on luggage and backpacks over our shoulders, we entered the terminal and followed behind people who we hoped knew where they were going.

There was a military presence at the airport, with a few soldiers carrying AK-47 machine guns. We were definitely in a different culture. Security in Canada is highly technical and sophisticated; you don't see military personnel carrying machine guns in the open public. The army's presence made me feel uneasy. I had never been to a Communist country. Having been born and nurtured in a democracy and not having traveled to many countries, I was not comfortable with armed security so in my face. Customs was quick and efficient, checking over our documents and taking our pictures.

At the luggage carousels, the bomb-sniffing dogs looked at Lily. Knowing how much of an animal lover she is, I cautioned her,

"Lily, these are working dogs. You can't try to get their attention and pet them."

"I know; they're doing their jobs."

"Yeah, the guys with the machine guns probably wouldn't appreciate it, and you don't want to get the dogs in trouble."

Heading out of the other side of the airport, luggage in tow, we were greeted by a long line of parked tour buses. It was sunny and hot. Although it's winter to the Cubans, I'm hit with waves of tropical heat that my pale skin hasn't felt in months. We were headed to the Memories Flamenco Beach Resort, on a fine white sandy beach with swimming pools, a waterfall, nightly entertainment, and highly recommended dining. After talking to others and doing research, we found out that food quality is a concern in Cuba. The food ratings and overall star rating for this resort were above average, which made me feel confident and comfortable with our decision to stay there.

The girls and I hopped onto one of the tour buses and took the only route out of the airport along a well-paved road through dense mangrove forests. Category 5 hurricane Irma ripped through this area six months prior to our trip when thousands of Canadian and European tourists were evacuated from the Jardines Del Rey area. From the tour bus window, I saw the resulting devastation on the surrounding landscape. Irma's terrible force caught the world off guard as people watched and prayed for all those in its path. Along the road to the resort, we saw mangrove trees with huge tangles of roots ripped out of the ground. While small patches of forest were blown over. In the path where the wind swirled, trees were broken apart and lying sideways in unison. Although I researched tourist reviews and blogs about the area post-Irma, I was still worried about the condition of the resort we were soon walking into.

This trip could not have come at a better time for educating Olivia and Lily on the real differences in life and culture in other parts of the world. Olivia was near the middle of her last semester of high school. We carefully booked this time to go on vacation as she was in between exams and large projects. We couldn't disrupt her very important schoolwork, especially when she had to maintain her grades for acceptance into one of the three Universities to which she applied. Olivia is a very studious person. At that time, she was getting great grades with a high overall grade point average. She attended a special University-sponsored high school program geared towards leadership and public speaking. A large amount of Olivia's packing space was taken up with textbooks, notebooks, binders, and other school supplies. Lily, equally doing well in school, was in grade six. Still, in elementary school, the pressure of projects, assignments, and tests was not nearly the same.

Our resort was one of the last stops of many. When it finally came into view, the entire bus full of snowbirds stopped talking; it was stunning. A majority of the damage caused by the hurricane had been repaired. There was a great amount of new landscaping being done around the resort. Newly planted trees were apparent all over the resort grounds where once mature trees probably stood. Maintenance on the ground floor sections of the buildings where flooding would have occurred were still being completed with new exterior trim and paint. For the most part, the resort was in good shape and esthetically welcoming. After retrieving our luggage, we stepped into the pleasant lobby decorated with a tropical vibe, alive with steel drum music playing and buzzing with activity. The rest of the day and Wednesday, we relaxed around the resort. While Lily and I roamed the resort at our leisure, Olivia lay poolside, taking up two lounge chairs —one chair for sunbathing and the other for all her books and readings. Olivia loved to tan and stayed in the same place under the sun for extended periods of time. Every once in a while, her book notes and binders would have to move so her tan could even out. We swam in the Caribbean, where the girls tasted their first mouthful of salt water, after which the pool was the favored swimming destination. Eating when hungry, taking in a couple of nighttime shows, meeting some locals, and relaxing on the beach completed our day.

On Wednesday afternoon, I began to feel like I had eaten something that wasn't agreeing with my digestive system. I was having bouts of diarrhea that concerned me. I didn't want to ruin my vacation. I became very cautious, strictly drinking bottled water and eating only foods I recognized that were obviously hot-- not sitting around for hours. I felt I was able to drink enough fluids to compensate for my condition. Hoping I would feel better soon, we decided to book an excursion for Friday on a jeep safari trip into the mountainous regions of Cuba. There were plenty of excursions to choose from, but this one seemed a good fit for exploring Cuban culture more closely by traveling through small towns, villages, and cities. The excursion would take us through forests and rivers and up into the low-lying mountains towards the center of the country. We would then ride in the mountains on horses, travel to a city for lunch, and continue to ride speedboats through mangrove forests, then return to the resort in the early evening. It sounded like the perfect fit for our family.

On Thursday, the girls and I decided to leave the resort area and go for an exploratory walk. The beach of white sand and finely crushed seashells was soft on our feet. Beside our resort was an estuary of greenery with mangrove trees surrounding small bodies of water. Penetrating into the waterways was difficult, but it was a perfect resting ground for flocks of flamingos. Along the beach, small rivers ran away from the estuary and into the blue waters of the Caribbean. The base of these small rivers was dark, squishy clay. As our feet sank into it, laughter bubbled from us as the slippery, cool clay slid between our toes. Continuing on our beach journey, we came across tide pools. Numerous clam mounds with little holes on top crested the water's surface, and tiny blue crabs staggered sideways through the shallows.

We travelled quite a distance, having rounded a corner, and we were no longer in eyesight of our resort. The sun was at its peak, and it was hot. We're having a great time exploring, but I was apprehensive about continuing much further, thinking about how much time it would take to get back to the resort. We had sunscreen on to protect our pasty white Canadian winter tans but didn't have any drinking water, hats, or shade to retreat to.

My legs started to feel heavy. *It must be walking in the sand.* It was giving me a good workout. I decided it was time to head back to the resort. The wind was no longer at our back; instead, we headed into it, a welcome relief from the heat. I enjoyed watching my daughter's long flowing hair dance behind them, a picturesque day with my two lovely daughters. We walked along the beautiful beach in solitude, with the turquoise waters of the Caribbean stretching as far as I could see behind us. It was a joyous moment as a proud dad, and I felt blessed to have such a beautiful family and the opportunity to share this time with them.

However, not long after we turned to head back to the resort, I started having difficulty walking. My legs, tired from what I thought was a good workout from walking through the sand, now felt like I was dragging heavy weights around my ankles. I have walked into strong winds before where I needed extra strength and momentum to push me forward, but the wind this day is not nearly at that velocity. My once long strides taking me back to the resort became labored like I was walking up a mountainside.

My breathing changed. I felt the need to take deep breaths of air as if I were racing mountain bikes in the steep terrain of coastal British Columbia.

Olivia and Lily continued in their regular pace back towards the resort, hair flowing, warm wind against their faces, and every so often arms out wide, basking in the day's glory. As they were forging ahead, I fell behind. They did not realize my difficulty. I slowed down and, at times, stopped to catch my breath. I had no idea what was going on with my health, and all I could think about was making it back to the resort under my own power. I had to stop walking and try to regroup. I knew I was having some trouble with diarrhea over the past day; the sun was hot, and we were out on the beach for what seemed a couple hours. I had sunstroke before when I was younger, and I knew the heat could affect me more harshly than others. *Perhaps I am just too overheated and fighting dehydration,* I thought. As I slowed down and rested my breathing, Olivia and Lily came back towards me.

By the time they returned, I had regained my breath, "Hey girls, I'm not feeling great. Don't know what it is, maybe the sun, not sure. I'm just going to take it slow, and when we get back to the resort, I'm going to lay down for a while and rest."

"Ok, Dad. We will walk slower and stick together more."

"For a while there, I felt like I just needed to sit down and rest. My legs were heavy. So, it would make me feel better if we stuck closer to each other."

The rest of the walk back along the beach resumed to normal. Whatever episode I had gone through had passed. I regained myself and made it back to the room, but I was shaken by what just happened. *A very unusual situation and not something I had ever encountered before,* I thought. *Best I just rest for the afternoon and perhaps evening. We have a big day planned tomorrow, and I want the day to go perfect and have the experience of a lifetime with my kids. I will rest today so I don't jeopardize tomorrow!*

Lily on the beach

Friday, Early Morning Adventure

Multiple alarms went off simultaneously at 6 a.m., and then the phone rang with a wake-up call from the resort. The day of our excursion was here. Knowing 6 a.m. is a time we are seldom awake and coherent, and we made sure we were ready to go the night before. We were only going to be gone for one day of fun, so we packed one backpack with snacks, a little bit of spending money, passports, travel insurance documents, phones, water, feminine products, and toilet paper. The room was quiet as we shuffled methodically, getting ready. It is as if we had practiced the drill of rising and leaving the room dozens of times leading up to this morning. We didn't take long getting out of the room, and we were off to the restaurant for an early morning meal before the long day ahead.

Our usual waitress stood near the entrance of the restaurant, happily greeting and escorting us to the section of service. Over the last couple of days, we had gotten to know our servers as every time we showed up, the two ladies would steer us to their section. Being a waiter, I am always one to tip well. I know how much tips mean to me and the well-being of my family, so I always like to return the service industry in kind. The two servers are especially nice to us and always make sure we are well looked after. I always put extra money on the table before we left for the day and never needed or wanted anything during our dining experience. The early Friday morning of the excursion was no different than our usual great service. There are not many guests in the dining room at this early hour, and we have most of the place to ourselves.

"Good morning, lovely family. Today is early for you, no?" She asks as she pours us some juice and water.

"Yes, quite a bit earlier than we are used to. Today we are going on an excursion. We are taking the jeeps to the mountains."

"Ah, very nice, you will have a good time. Looks like it be a nice day for you. Will you be back in time for dinner?"

"We are having lunch in Moron, then a boat ride, and then back to the resort, so we should be here for dinner."

"I'm working tonight, so I look for you and find you a seat."

The day before was a tough and unusual day for me, and I wanted to make sure I didn't overindulge in food to disrupt my bowels any more than they already were. I ate very light, with just fruit and bread. I drink only juice and have my bottled water with me. I am being very cautious with everything I put into my body today.

It was a beautiful sunny morning with blue skies and a few white scattered clouds. The tour bus arrived late as it had a few stops before us at other resorts. The bus was fairly new and had nice, comfortable seats and air conditioning. A young lady with straight, long, dark brown hair and tanned skin stood up at the front of the bus and introduced herself with a slight Spanish accent.

"Hello everybody, my name is Rosemary. Rose, like the flower, and Mary like the virgin...but not really," she said with a laugh. Everyone had a bit of a laugh along with her, and this brought the energy level up to start the day right on such an early morning.

Rosemary commanded attention with her voice and upbeat positivity. "We are sorry we are a bit late, so we are going to move quickly to our first destination."

The bus jerked forward, and the sound of the transmission wound high before the driver changed gears, departing fast from the resort.

Rosemary grabbed onto a couple of the seats to steady herself as the bus roared forward and swerved around corners. She continued, "We are going to have a fantastic day. We are now heading to the staging area, where we will receive our jeeps for the day. There will be four people per jeep, and you must pick a driver. The driver must be able to drive a standard transmission, also known as a stick shift. No lazy drivers on this trip; you must work for it!

If you are having any trouble along the route, something with the vehicle, or any emergency, pull over to the side of the road and push the button for the four-way flashers, the emergency lights. We will have a lead car and a car at the back as well, and we will get to you as soon as possible."

The jeeps were lined up along the side of the road leading out of a chained-in compound. These were not the type we usually see in North America. The jeeps were not the trademark GM off-road vehicles but rather smaller Japanese Suzuki off-road vehicles. The Suzuki's hard tops were a blessing as I worried about constant sun exposure throughout the day. Four people to a jeep, and we are a group of three. There were no single people on this excursion, so we lucked out and had a jeep to ourselves. I had owned a couple of manual transmission cars before, but it had been at least 15 years since I last drove one. The jeeps are all black except for the lead jeep driven by our tour guide, which was red. Inspecting the jeeps, I noticed they were all a bit newer, so I figured that the clutch was probably easier than older model manual cars that I had driven. I also noticed there were countless scratches in the paint. I figured we must be headed for some close-quarter driving through brush.

On the first leg of the trip to the horseback riding ranch in the mountains, we agreed that Olivia, being the oldest, would ride in the front and Lily would have the back seat to herself. After the ranch, we would switch the two girls to allow Lily some time in the front with me. Our starting position for this leg of the trip was the third vehicle from the front. Nervously, I depress the clutch, put the transmission in first gear, and slowly press on the accelerator while simultaneously releasing the clutch. The jeep moved forward, and I had to quickly shift into second, then third. I make it to the first stop at the intersection leading out of the jeep compound. I did not want to stall and embarrass myself in front of another seven cars. I eased the clutch and gas pedal again and shot out onto the main road leading towards the manmade causeway linking Cayo Coco to the city of Moron. Although the clutch was easy to navigate, the ride was very rough and shaky.

At moderate to high speeds, the steering wheel shook tremendously. It was like a ball joint was shot, and finding fifth gear was a real test of patience and precision. Several times, I just gave up trying to find the fifth gear—as I would need a small sledgehammer to slam the gear shift into place—and I drove the car in fourth. I knew we were going to be in for a rough ride, and at the end of the day, I suspected I would be completely exhausted from fighting with the steering and transmission. The drive across the causeway was pretty, with shallow saltwater estuaries on either side of the road. It is home to many different types of birds we had never seen in our northern country. The water was a beautiful turquoise color. I shifted the transmission properly and as smoothly as possible. The girls smiled as they felt the freedom of being away from the tourist resorts.

On the other side of the causeway, we passed through a toll booth and checkpoint, entering the mainland of Cuba. Travel documents ready, it was a seamless entry as this group of tourist jeeps took the same route a couple of times a day every day of the week. Once through the toll gate, we veer off the main road and head onto a secondary road, driving straight through a small town.

We were able to see what I had wanted Olivia and Lily to see and experience: the different conditions of the Cuban people living in the country as opposed to tourist urban centers. Very small and damaged houses lined the streets made up of wood, cinderblocks, and plaster walls. The roofs were typically sheet metal or clay. Some of the homes only had half a roof and no doors or windows. Each was very small, and some homes were not much larger than a standard bedroom. The houses contained surrounding property, small gardens planted, and laundry hanging out to dry. Although I wanted to take the time to look and take in my surroundings, I needed to keep aware of my driving as chickens and dogs freely roam the streets. Roosters strutted around with their necks jutting backward and forwards and held themselves high like they were the kings of the world. I envy the relaxed nature of this community and a more natural and unconfined order.

Most locals greeted us as our procession of jeeps traveled through their communities. Older women sat on their porches and front gardens waving and smiling. Young women with children wrapped in their arms perked up at our arrival through their town, and others emerged out to the side of the road to watch us drive by. There were very few young men to be seen. The men must have been in the surrounding fields or small industrial operations and businesses. Children emerged from between houses and buildings, ran to the road, and greeted us with big smiles and waves as we passed by. Having the positive attention of the locals made us feel important like we were part of a parade.

Driving around and then through this hamlet, we exited onto a paved country road. A few minutes down this road, I followed the lead jeeps with a right turn into an open field through a gap in a fence. The smooth pavement of the road made way for a makeshift, unmaintained dirt road that cut across an open field to an entrance into a dense green forest.

The ground beneath our jeep was like stationary ocean waves of dirt. There was more than one set of tracks to navigate. Watching the jeep bounce and descend into deep pits, I constantly switched which track was the lesser of two evils.

Olivia and I were strapped in with front shoulder belts, but Lily was in the back with an open bench seat and only a lap belt around her waist. I worried about the little support she had from the back and forth, up and down of the jeep through this washed-out road. Olivia, in the passenger seat, had one hand locked tight on the interior door handle and the other outstretched towards the front dash to support any sudden forward movement.

I looked back at Lily, and she was having a great time with arms stretched out to either side, trying to grab hold of anything that could steady her and support her from slamming into the interior. She was on an amusement park ride that she didn't have to wait in line for; there was no end in sight, and she had the seat to herself. At eleven years old, Lily can navigate the back seat for a little while without getting hurt. This excursion was a full day, and I was truly hoping the lack of a proper road would eventually smooth out. In the meantime, everyone was able to stay safe. Anxiety over how safe and secure everyone feels eventually gave way to laughter. We were having a blast.

After weaving around natural rock and dirt obstacles, we finally made our way into the forest. The makeshift road flattened, the jeep procession started to speed up, and we drove through a magnificent, dense mixed forest while threading the needle between two everglade ecosystems on either side. The single roadway was made even tighter by encroaching vegetation. A number of times, the jeeps were bushwhacking through overreaching branches from the surrounding trees. The tree branches scraped along the sides of the vehicles like fingernails on a chalkboard. Earlier, I had first inspected the jeeps in the compound and saw all the scratches, and I now knew where they came from. We traveled further and deeper along this dirt road that led beside this narrow, shallow body of water, Laguna la Glorieta.

Peering between the leaves and bushes rushing past our jeep, we saw large numbers of snowy egrets feeding in the shallow, rich waters. In this seemingly untouched area, we saw a number of butterflies glide past our jeep. The more we pressed on, the more butterflies appeared. The jeeps before us must have disturbed the resting butterflies. The air was suddenly filled with hundreds of delicate insects.

Back home in Canada, when Olivia and Lily were younger, we made several trips to butterfly emporiums. The large, enclosed greenhouse contained exotic plants, streams, waterfalls, and of course, a huge number of exotic delicate butterflies. We would purposefully wear bright-colored clothing, knowing the butterflies would be attracted to us and our chances of them landing on us would dramatically increase. It was amazing to see many of the same species of butterflies that we had seen in captivity, now in the wild: Swallowtails, Cuban Kings, Zebra Longwings, Sleepy Oranges, and one of our favorites, the large Blue Morpho with owl eyespots on the wing undersides, and as the wing opens a vibrant, iridescent blue shines and reflects in the sunlight.

Most of the butterflies ride the airstream around our jeep and avoid getting squished on our windshield, but a number of them, mostly the smaller and more numerous Sleepy Orange species, did not make it. We all feel devastated. Olivia and I, aware of the feelings of Lily in the backseat, just kept repeating loudly, "it's the circle of life," hoping to ease the empathy she has towards her insect friends.

Pressing onward along the beat-up trail, we came to a halt as the lead vehicle had stopped due to a downed tree crossing our path. The tour guides brought wood saws from the rear of their vehicle and started immediately cutting the tree branches so we could push forward. I had the feeling we were behind schedule as the lead jeep was constantly pushing the caravan of tourists hard and fast through these unfamiliar roads. This downed tree is not helping us. After five minutes of cutting the smaller branches, we drove on skirting around the remaining large trunk.

Rain showers had been intermittent that week, with dark rogue clouds deeply concentrated with rain streaming over the resort, and it was overall a pleasant break from the sun and heat. The rain had a significant impact on the typography of the route we were taking as we came to the crossing of a large flowing stream. The lead jeep came to a halt in order to assess the best route across the water. I thought about the trip we had already taken, the impossibly narrow trail we had just traversed. There was no way we could navigate our jeeps into a turn and retrace our route back.

I was a pretty confident driver and imagined having to navigate our jeep in reverse the whole way back. I reminisced about a story that my stepfather told us regarding one of his crazy friends from his youth who decided that he was going to have a "backward" day. He was going to drive the whole day in reverse, which he did around his neighborhood throughout his daily routine to stores, friends' places, and just cruising for enjoyment.

After a few minutes of assessing the river, the driver of the lead jeep had figured out the best route forward. I am relieved my driving backward skills are not to be tested.

Large boulders are underneath the rushing water, and the lead jeep found a couple of them, making the jeep bounce sideways. By the time it was our turn to cross, a definite safe passage route was created for us to take. The water was high. On the jeep before us, we can see the water reaching past the floorboards and flowing slightly above the door seam. I had to make sure I concentrated on the path everyone took as it was not a good spot to waver and get stuck in the middle of fast-moving water. I had never crossed moving water so deep before, and the girls and I were quite excited and a bit nervous at the same time. We held on tightly to both the jeep and our breaths, and within a few seconds of splashing, water rushed alongside the jeep and hit the windshield; we were through and on the other side. Joyous laughter, as well as the never-ending jarring and movement of our torsos flailing around the jeep, tightened our abdomens. We are ready and hoping for some physical relief with smoother driving ahead as we wait for the others to cross.

Jeep excursion. Crossing a river

After a few jeeps had found the right path through the water, and with no time to waste, the lead jeep jumped ahead on its journey, enticing the line of straggling jeeps with it. After a couple more kilometers and a quick couple of turns on the trail, we headed out of the forested everglade area.

The trees became scarce, and we found ourselves driving along a country road better suited for horse and buggy travel.

Without the larger tires and higher clearance of the jeeps, there is no way anyone could traverse these country roads. Eventually, to the physical delight of our bodies, the road flattened to a steady rock-lined access road.

With the forest far behind us, the geography we were traveling through became ranch land: Barren, dusty fields with rusted wire fences stretched on either side of us for as far as we could see. The landscape we were driving through could have been taken out of any old Western movie. The homesteads were much larger and more well-built and maintained than the housing that we had seen closer to more populated towns. Seemingly, the ranchers had more resources and a slightly better financial position.

As we continued through this straight-out-of-western movie landscape, we crossed paths with groups of working ranchers on horseback. Clothed in dirty, thick leather chaps, cowboy boots, and the nostalgic western cowboy hat, these guys did not move a muscle to crack a greeting smile. Straight-faced, sideway glances were all we received. We were definitely not welcomed, as we had been in the towns, and felt as if we were encroaching on their land. Perhaps the iron horses we were driving were trespassing on their turf and disrupting the natural flow of their environment. These were obviously hard-working men by the state of their clothes, leathered look of their skin, and squinted eyes from the constant brightness of the hot day sun. By contrast, we were a train of bright-colored, clean-clothed, funny hat-wearing, sunglass, and jewelry-bedazzled tourists passing through their day. Nope, I definitely did not feel we were welcome.

The dirt and fist-sized boulder-laden road continued for a number of kilometers. The suspension on the jeep was being put through the wringer, and the vibration from the road was transferring up through the steering wheel. After many kilometers of continuous arm rattling and vibration through the steering column, I thought my arms were going to fall off. The landscape was dry and void of any greenery. It was hard to imagine anything living out here, plant or animal. After driving the rough road in the middle of nowhere, the ground started to smooth out to a hard-packed dirt, and houses came into view. We entered the small town of Falla. The houses were the same small self-constructed homes with tin or clay tiled roofs, open-air windows, some with wrought iron bars, numerous clotheslines, and animals such as chickens, cats, and dogs roamed around. Something new was individual cows tied up to large stakes in the ground near the drainage ditches opposite the homes. Not every home had a cow. For these people, possessing one cow could have made a huge difference to their livelihoods and perhaps the livelihoods of their neighbors or extended family.

The lead jeep sped along and turned off the main road again, taking us on a country road that seemed like it was once a railway line past numerous flat farming fields until our next populated area, the small city of Chambas.

Friday Late Morning, the Horses

We finally met a paved road!

The city of Chambas is situated on elevated ground with a river stretching from its eastern edge. Approaching Chambas along an abandoned and uprooted rail line, we crossed the river on an old, converted train bridge. The passing water was far below the bridge, hinting that it was quite an old river that had carved its existence over many centuries. Entering the southeastern edge of Chambas, we drove up a short, steep hill to some of the main structures of the city. This stretch of road on the southern edge of the city housed some small businesses, as well as a central bus terminal and some government offices.

The largest and notably the most expensive and well-cared-for architectural construction was an official-sized baseball stadium. It was hard to grasp the contrast of this elaborately manicured stadium amongst the surrounding archaic and dilapidated municipal infrastructures. The stadium seating surrounded beautiful green turf and meticulously groomed red dirt infield. The streets were crowded with other vehicles and people offloading trucks on the sides of the road. Paying attention to the road, we did not have time to look around. We quickly got to the edge of the city and back onto the dirt road that was heading into a statuesque green forested mountain range. The ranch we were headed to was nestled in a mountain range between the cities of Chambas and Florencia known as Canon de la Lagunas, Canyon of the Lagoons. The road entering this valley between the mountains was a well-traveled dirt road. The uneven road was, at some points, very slow going. Without an off-road vehicle, driving to this ranch would have been nearly impossible. The canopy of trees rose up on either side of us, and we eventually emerged into a hidden valley of agricultural land. The jeeps pulled into a semicircle, and we were all relieved to be able to get out and put our feet on solid ground after the grueling, stressful, yet fun three-and-a-half-hour drive.

Lily on her horse at the Cuban ranch

Overlooking the ranch.

Horse ranch in the mountains

The ranch was an extensive property with many outbuildings. We were told the operation was very successful, and it showed with the available amenities such as plumbing and working bathrooms. The main home on the property is large by Cuban standards, made of concrete walls and ceramic tile floors, which kept it quite cool in the tropical heat. A gentle breeze flowed through the home, bringing in the fresh scent of fields and pine forests. The main house entrance had a covered breezeway that attached to a row of livestock stables. A donkey and its foal greeted us as well as a litter of kittens and the ever-present running chickens. Olivia and Lily, true animal lovers, were delighted to share some time with new animal friends.

We were told there would be time for relaxation and refreshments after our horseback ride and before we continued on to our lunch destination in the city of Moron. On the front yard of the property, there were at least 30 horses lined up, saddled with western saddles, and ready for their passengers. I had been around horses for many years as my mother grew up with them from a young age and has had horses off and on for the past 60 years. Olivia and Lily had the pleasure of being exposed to horses at Grandma and Papa's house. But these ranch horses are the size of ponies. Much smaller in stature than what we are accustomed to in Canada. Most of the horses were either very thin, very old, or both. The horses were quiet and easy to mount, like they had been doing this same routine their entire lives. Many on our tour needed assistance getting up into their saddles. Olivia and Lily knew the proper way to mount a horse and slung their leg over the saddles with ease. Waiting patiently while the rest of the group attempted to climb aboard their four-legged transportation, Lily slowly and gently brushed the reins up and down the neck of her horse. The horse seemed to enjoy the scratch from her passenger, settled, and stood still amongst the jittery commotion of the other horses. Lily relaxed in the saddle and felt a trusted bond with her riding companion, elevating her confidence in the ride ahead. After everyone mounted, we rode slowly down the driveway to the dirt road, following the guides.

Each horse has its place in the herd, and no matter how much coaxing you did, it didn't seem to matter. The horses knew what to do better than the rider and fell into their places accordingly. Lily's small horse liked to be at the front of the pack and took off weaving through the herd until I lost sight of her, and she made it to the front with the lead rancher guide. Olivia's horse also moved quickly through the herd of thirty-plus horses until I lost sight of her, and she made it toward the middle of the pack. My horse went at its own slow pace, withdrew to the rear of the pack, and held onto that position regardless of how much I tried to get it moving. I preferred the idea of riding with my girls, but eventually gave up trying and tried to relax and enjoy the ride. At least I was out of the jeep and not fighting the difficult transmission and clanging suspension. My horse kept getting closer and closer to the horse in front of us. Eventually, it was so close that my horse's nose was buried in the tail of the one preceding us. It seemed rather inappropriate to me, but that was where it felt comfortable, and the other horse didn't seem to mind too much.

The herd of horses stretched out quite far, and in the more open farm fields, I could see Olivia and Lily riding towards the front of the pack. Lily was right beside the guide's horse at the front, and she was comfortable and confident with her riding. This was the first time I had seen Lily so independent. It was one of those proud parenting moments where you see your child grow up in front of your eyes. Olivia was already at the age of independence—she usually spent more time away from us than with us—favoring friendships and independent study. Lily was still very much a child to us and needed taking care of and nurturing. Seeing her so far away from me at the front of the group handling a horse and feeling comfortable socializing around strangers was enlightening.

She is growing up and becoming a young woman, I thought.

It didn't seem long before we were at the ranch again. Olivia and Lily headed towards the house so they could have time with the donkey and kittens and enjoy refreshments before heading back to the jeeps.

Our next destination is the city of Moron, where we are to have a traditional Cuban lunch at one of the first independently-owned restaurants in Cuba. I figured they purposefully chose to highlight this restaurant as it was an opportunity to showcase a loosening of the Communist country's regime on entrepreneurism. Regardless of any political propaganda or showboating, the tour group had a difficult and stressful time driving all morning, and the consensus was we were all extremely hungry and looked forward to sitting down once again after another long drive ahead.

Olivia, Lily, and I found access to the rooftop of the barn. Standing on the rooftop overlooking the valley and the steep incline to the tree-lined mountains around us, we looked at our surroundings in quiet comfort, relishing in the bathing sun and tranquility.

"Hey Lily, you really took off there on that horse," I said.

"Yeah, it was fun. My horse really wanted to get to the front, and she was fast."

"Did you have trouble staying on? Was the horse smooth, and did you feel scared at all?" I couldn't help asking.

"Nope, not at all. I was fine. I just hung on tight. I didn't expect to go to the front, but the horse really wanted to be up there. It was neat riding with the head cowboy."

Olivia spoke up, "My horse was pretty good too. I couldn't make him go much faster. He just stayed in the middle of the pack. I tried to get him going faster to catch up to Lily, but he wouldn't."

I laughed and said, "Same with mine. My horse's nose stuck into the butt of the one in front of me and just stayed there. I couldn't get it moving any faster. I was kind of embarrassed. I kept trying to move him off to the side out of the ass of the other horse, but he kept going back." The lady on the horse in front looked back at us, and all I could do was shrug, letting her know that I tried but he seemed to like where he was."

Lily and Olivia laughed at my misfortune.

Rosemary and the rest of the guides gathered everyone's attention to get back to the jeeps as we were running late. "The drive to Moron is about 40 kilometers, and getting from the ranch to the main road in Chambas is going to take some time," Rosemary warned us.

Without thinking and as a result of habit, Olivia naturally got into the front passenger seat of the jeep while Lily took the back. But before we left the jeep compound in the morning, it was agreed that Olivia would take the front seat for half the trip, and Lily would then switch to the front seat for the drive to Moron. It wasn't until we were on our way that I remembered this agreement. We were moving at a rapid pace behind the lead car with no time to stop. It didn't seem like Lily remembered the seating agreement, so I just left it alone. I figured we would switch after we had our lunch at the restaurant, and I would not mention it until then.

Exiting the mountain range, we connected with a paved road. Once our jeeps were bunched in a line back through the southern edge of Chambas, the lead jeep jolted into a rapidly increasing pace. Our group was late, and the speed of the lead jeep was making it known. None of the group knew which way we were to go. All we knew was that we were headed to the city of Moron. The lead jeep drove so fast that we lost sight of him. We need to step it up. The guide was passing vehicles at high speed, passing public transportation buses on uphill sections of the road, and not relenting his speed to anything before him. It was definitely scary trying to keep up with him, and taking risky chances seemed necessary in order to keep up.

Halfway from Chambas and the next town, Calvario, the lead jeep resumed a more normal speed where the rest of the jeeps rode in unison. We reached rural and agricultural land, and I pointed out to Olivia and Lily the manual labor taking place with regard to the cutting, stacking, and lifting of the sugar cane onto old transportation work trucks. Around our home in Brantford, Ontario, we have many farms. Most of the farms are industrial-size operations that are cultivated and tended using heavy machinery. One sees very little physical labor other than the operation of large tractors and combines. The sugar cane here was being harvested manually with widely swinging arms and hands holding machetes. Working in bare feet did not seem uncommon. Large-rimmed straw hats were the only protection these workers had from the hot sun. The working men of the sugar cane fields were all thin with wiry, muscled arms. Even as we drove past these workers at a fast pace, we saw the glistening sweat off their bodies. My heart sunk with empathy towards them, knowing that most of these workers did not have a choice of profession. Generation after generation, they fell into the same life of hard back-breaking work with little to no financial gain.

Passing through the towns of Calvario, Crucero, Falla, and Ranchuelo towards Moron was a relaxing downtime on a well-paved road. The interior of our jeep is quiet except for the hum of the tires and rattling of our front suspension as we each fell into our own thoughts as we passed this foreign landscape. We had seen and experienced much, and it was nice to be able to sit back and enjoy the ride. There was a calmness in the jeep as we drove along the Avenida Antonio Guiteras eastward towards Moron. Approaching Moron, we passed large stretches of rural agricultural lands. Storm ditches were along the sides of the roads, and colorful wildflowers grew on the embankments separating the roads from the fields. The landscape was picturesque and calming.

Friday Sun Overhead, the Vibration

As the wildflowers and fields passed by on our way into Moron, I felt content with my daughters and looked forward to future adventures.

Suddenly, a small vibration started in my chest.

It was distinct from the vibration of the vehicle that we had been feeling throughout the day; this vibration was coming from inside me, in the area of my heart.

I had felt fluttering from heart palpitations a number of times before near the height of my mountain bike racing. I had my heart checked because of an irregular heartbeat that was causing me problems of anxiety and panic attacks. The diagnosis explained to me that my heart was very efficient and didn't need to pump as much. My lower heart chamber would skip a beat, filling the chamber with excess blood. Once released, this extra volume thrust of blood gave me a bit of a head rush, threw off my blood pressure, and then sent my body into counter measures against what it mistakenly perceived as a heart attack. I would feel lightheaded and flushed, and my breathing would be labored. I was told that my body would have to self-regulate after an episode like this and that it usually took about 20 minutes to do so. After the doctor's result and a lengthy stress test, I was cleared to resume my everyday life. This type of episode did not happen very often, but when it did, I knew what was happening and could mentally adapt and prepare to feel uncomfortable for the next 20 minutes.

I was told my body would take a few years to adapt and get used to the irregular heartbeats, and things would get better over time, and they did. The palpitations would be few and far between, only lasting a couple of seconds and routed away by an exaggerated cough to set things straight.

Unfortunately, the heart palpitation that started on our way into the city of Moron did not subside or go away upon several attempts to cough it out. The palpitations, which usually lasted a few seconds, never went beyond minutes. I was feeling very uncomfortable with the situation. As we continued to drive toward the city, I grew nervous and started to feel as if one of my panic attacks was about to reappear. I had not had one in years. Years ago, if I started having one of these episodes while driving, I would pull over and wait it out until it passed, or if Louise were with me, we would simply change drivers.

But traveling in a group of jeeps, I felt I didn't have that option, and I had to drive through it. I tried to relax and reached for the large bottle of water to take a few gulps. I started feeling flush, so I reached for the air conditioner and placed it on full blast with as many vents pointed toward me as possible. The palpitations were continuing. I knew this was not normal, and I felt I needed to say something to Olivia and Lily.

I turned to Olivia in the passenger seat and said, "I think I'm having an anxiety or panic attack. just wanted to let you know in case I need to pull over."

Olivia, being supportive and knowing my past, said, "Okay, no problem, just do what you need to do."

Buildings and Industry were replacing the open agricultural fields, and I knew we were getting close to the outer city limits. My breathing started to get deeper, and my mind was not as sharp as it should have been. I began to concentrate more on what was happening to me physically rather than what was in front of me. We approached a strange intersection on the outer limit of the city.

There was a train track to cross, then three directions to go right after. The lead jeep took the second turn. I knew my concentration was lost. The objects around me seemed to move slower. Tunnel vision was starting to set in, and I knew it was time to pull over and try to sort myself out before continuing on with our day. As much as I didn't want to stop and become the center of attention, I knew it was necessary for our safety.

I tried to pick out a safe spot to pull over. Again, there were chickens, dogs, and people walking the streets, and I needed to seize the first opportunity to find a place to stop. Half a block into the city, a clearing appeared at the side of the road. I quickly veered into the small clearing. I stopped the jeep. Darkness was creeping in around my vision. I placed the gear shift in neutral. Everything slowed down, and I knew I needed to hit the emergency lights to signal that I was in distress. It took all my concentration to reach out and press the red emergency button on the dash. The darkness closed around my vision. Everything went black.

Although I was able to place the vehicle in neutral, my foot was still resting heavily on the accelerator. The engine revved under the weight of my leg and foot. We still had forward momentum and were slowly heading towards a parked car in front of us. Olivia reached over to the steering wheel and turned it to disrupt the forward movement. The car stopped rolling. She then reached over the middle console to grab onto my leg and attempt to move it off the accelerator pedal. Her reach and angle were not good, and she couldn't muster the strength to lift my leg. Strange moans were exhaling out of me as I was slumped over and being held up by the seatbelt.

Lily, from the back seat, saw my skin collapse around my neck and change color. She started screaming. While trapped in the back, she turned towards the rear window and began to slam her small hand against the glass, screaming for help from another jeep in our group that had pulled up behind us.

Olivia said she yelled, trying to awaken me, and noticed that my complexion had turned red and my lips were becoming blue. I had stopped breathing. It took a while for people from the tour group to get out of their vehicles to come and see what was happening in our jeep. Just as Olivia was about to jump out of the car, someone from the jeep behind us approached and opened the driver's side door. Olivia, with panic in her voice, asked,

"Can you move his leg off the pedal because I can't?"

The man grabbed my leg and pulled my foot off the accelerator.

Olivia continued, "Is he breathing?"

The man said, "I don't know."

"Can you check? Because if he isn't, we need to do CPR."

The man checked and again said, "I don't know."

A minute had passed, and by then, a group of people had gathered at the side of our jeep, including Rosemary, the tour guide.

Olivia, not getting the answers she needed from the group of people, decided to take action to save my life and proceeded to reach for her door handle. Before she could get out of the jeep to run around to the driver's side, pull me out, and onto the ground, I had regained consciousness.

From the time I lost consciousness after pressing the emergency signal in the jeep to the time I regained consciousness, I do not remember anything. Everything had gone black; I had no recollection of anything, and I consciously lost a minute and a half of my life. My heart had obviously stopped functioning, and there was no resuscitation to counter or correct my condition. I should have stayed dead. Despite being in such poor condition, I was quite coherent when I came around. I looked out at the small crowd outside my door and stated that I was okay. The only reason that I could come up with was that I had an irregular heartbeat that threw off my blood pressure. It was the only thing that made sense to me.

Rosemary was on her phone to her superiors, relaying the situation that had just unfolded. When she saw that I had regained consciousness, she came over to my side and asked if I was okay and what had happened. I relayed a brief history of my past issues with irregular heartbeat, anxiety, blood pressure, etc.

Rosemary asked, "Well, are you okay to drive?"

Sitting for a few seconds without answering, I took a self-assessment of how I was feeling. Unfortunately, my heart was still fluttering, but I did not have the same anxiety or predisposition to pass out again.

"This has happened to me before, but not this bad," I said. I need some time for my body to regulate my blood pressure again, and I am not feeling quite good enough to drive. It usually takes about 25 minutes or so."

A man still kneeling beside the jeep, Pat, offered to drive our jeep for us to our next destination, the restaurant. "The hospital is only a few blocks away. It is a very good hospital, very close, very big. We can go there if you feel the need to." Rosemary said. "It will not be any trouble in case you want or need to get checked out."

I could sense that Rosemary was very concerned about what had happened and had my best interest at heart.

Not wanting to be that person to disrupt everyone's day even further, and my own stubbornness to not land in a Cuban hospital, I said, "I think I just need time, but if I feel I need to go to the hospital, I will let you know."

I knew I was not out of the woods yet as I could still feel fluttering around my heart. I got out of the driver's seat to let Pat, who was from Toronto, drive the rest of the way to the restaurant. I decided to sit in the back seat so I could spend less time concentrating on the road ahead and avoid as much conversation as possible while I gathered my thoughts on what just happened. I didn't want anyone to know I was still physically struggling, and my mind was reeling while thinking about what happened and what I was going to do next. I hoped the strange heart palpitation would just eventually go away like it always had in the past. If it would just correct itself, our day and the rest of our trip would return to normal like nothing had happened.

Pat was a kind man in his mid 50's. He was in a peculiar situation, stepping up and driving a car with complete strangers, but he was trying his best to start a conversation. I was thankful to have been in the back seat as Pat and Olivia struck up a conversation, thus relieving me from talking and allowing me to assess my situation.

Despite what had just happened and dealing with the continued palpitations, I continued to look out the window and take in the cultural sights of this small city. I couldn't help but notice the streets were becoming narrower. The buildings and houses were tightly knit and beautifully displayed early 20th-century Spanish Colonial architecture. Stucco-wrapped cinder block construction with large rectangular and arched windows and large decorative columns on the ground floor rise to a second floor with wooden slatted window shutters. The structures were painted in earth tones with white, yellow ochre, and burnt sienna. There are some buildings with light blue and green as well. Painted intricate ironwork covered many of the doors and windows.

Some of the structures have hints of late Baroque influence with decorative columns and Baroque design elements on the facades of the buildings. After driving in a typical grid-like pattern of right and left turns, we eventually ended up in the northeastern end of the city. The restaurant where we were scheduled for lunch was El Pino Atrevido. We had been brought to this restaurant purposefully to showcase one of the first privately owned businesses in Communist Cuba. This restaurant was an exception to Communist ideology and was being put on display for the tourists. There was street parking only. The line of ten jeeps pulled up one behind the other on the narrow road in front of the restaurant. Approaching the restaurant, my heart was still not in a normal rhythm.

Rosemary approached me from across the road and asked again, "Are you okay"?

I reply, "I don't feel like I am going to faint again, but I still do not feel normal as the palpitations are continuing in my chest. I am okay, but I still need some time."

The restaurant was open air, which meant no air conditioning, and it was hot outside. The exterior of the restaurant was walled with tile and decorative white colonial fencing and a roof structure constructed with thatched palm leaves. Entering the iron gate door, I headed to the nearest table, wasting no time sitting down.

I felt exhausted and overwhelmed by what had just happened. My heart was still out of rhythm, but I was still functioning. I decided to order a can of bubbly limeade. With this heat, I reasoned, perhaps something cold would help how I was feeling.

Once settled, I tell Olivia and Lily that I am headed to the bathroom.

It was a small bathroom, and the door didn't shut properly. The sink was a beautiful mosaic of yellow and blue decorative tiles. I need to get away from everyone for a while and try to compose myself, correct my slightly exaggerated breathing, and hopefully, my out-of-rhythm heart. I splashed water on my face, took large calming breaths, and tried to cough and disrupt my heart and reset the rhythm. Nothing worked. It was a blue-skied sunny hot day, but I was not sure my sweating was because of the heat. I'm normally not a sweater by nature, but nervousness and anxiety were getting the better of me.

I had been in the bathroom for a lot longer than normal; Olivia nervously knocked on the half-opened door. "Dad, how are you doing?" She asked.

Not letting on that the palpitations were continuing, I replied, "Okay, but still not feeling well. I'm not feeling like I am going to faint again. I'm still going to be in here a few minutes freshening up. I won't be too much longer. I will come out to join you at the table as soon as I'm done."

Seemingly satisfied, Olivia said, "Okay, I just wanted to check on you," and left to join Lily at the table.

I continued to splash water on my face to cleanse the perspiration. Realizing that staying in the bathroom was not going to help the situation, I needed to get back to Olivia and Lily as they were sitting by themselves waiting for me. I left the bathroom and returned to the table with the girls.

Seeing I had returned, Rosemary, generally concerned with my well-being, approached me and assured me that it wouldn't be a problem taking me to the hospital to get checked and that the hospital was not very far away.

Again, being stubborn and probably frustrating my guardian angel to no end, I said, "Thank you, but I would like to give it some more time, and I will let you know soon either way."

Concerned, Rosemary exclaimed, "You know we do still have some boats to go on after this."

"Yes, I know. Perhaps I could just sit out of the activity at the docks and just rest. Thank you for your concern. I really do appreciate it. I will think about the hospital and let you know."

People from the tour group started towards the traditional Cuban lunch buffet. I went up to the buffet and had a look at the offering but did not feel any appetite whatsoever. I decided the bubbly drink was enough. Olivia nor Lily had much of an appetite either. They each took a token amount of food to be polite but did not eat much. We were quiet at the table, and we didn't talk much as it would have been awkward to speak about me fainting, stopping breathing, and turning a different color. I was still feeling the palpitations of my heart.

Olivia told me that she had gotten in touch with Mom and that she was going to call back in a few minutes to talk with me. I looked forward to her call as usually she could rationally talk sense into a situation and ask the right questions. Sitting at the lunch table was surreal. I had a difficult time concentrating on my surroundings. I was keeping my mind on my heart, and going through my head were a number of scenarios, all of which were not desirable. I wanted to continue on with the day to the boats, but I would not be able to take part in the activity. I did not want to take the opportunity away from the girls to have fun the rest of the day. I know that if we are to leave the restaurant now, I will not feel safe driving as the palpitations are still happening. I definitely did not want to end up in a Cuban hospital.

Friday Evening, to the Hospital

I had, over the years, heard stories of third-world Island hospitals and, in my mind, pictured the worst conditions possible. I had a hard time maintaining eye contact with the girls, and I was incapable of any meaningful conversation. I was worried. I looked over towards Rosemary, sitting with the other guides, and her eyes were trained on me while she was busy on the phone. I felt like every eye was on me in the restaurant. Talk of me fainting and not breathing circulated through the other tour patrons, and I could sense and feel their eyes on me. I got sympathetic looks from our group at other tables, and as soon as they knew I was looking at them, they turned away. I just want to shrink into a corner somewhere and disappear. Olivia's phone rang, and it was Louise. The phone was handed to me, and it was a relief to hear her voice.

"Hi, Hon, how are you feeling?" she asked.

"I'm okay but not great. I started having palpitations and blacked out."

"I know. Olivia called me when you went to the bathroom and told me what happened. Are you still having the palpitations?"

"Yeah," I replied with a bit of defeat in my voice. "I'm still having palpitations. My heart doesn't feel right, feels like butterflies fluttering, but I don't feel like I'm going to faint again."

Louise, knowing and experiencing my past bouts of irregular heartbeats and anxiety, then asked, "How long has this been going on for?"

Not really realizing how much time had passed, I looked at my watch and made a good estimate of close to an hour since I had looked at my watch last when we were just entering the city.

"That's not normal. You know this situation in the past usually only lasted about twenty minutes, and that is a lot longer than twenty minutes. It is not anxiety. You are dealing with something much different, and you need to get it checked out."

"I know, it shouldn't have been this long; it should have gotten better by now." Louise then restated, "You need to get checked out. Olivia said there was a hospital nearby. You have to get it checked, you have to…promise me you will go and get it checked!" Louise's voice was adamant. Accepting her voice of reason, I know then I have no choice but to succumb to my Cuban hospital fears and get checked.

"I promise I will go," I stated.

The lunch was almost finished, and I told Louise that I would have Rosemary, the tour guide, take me as soon as everyone was finished at the restaurant.

"I love you!"

Louise returned, "I love you too, and keep in touch!"

"I will. Do you want to speak to Olivia?"

I passed the phone to Olivia so they could finish the conversation and plan to stay in touch.

I had a hard time focusing on anything except the fluttering in my chest and what it meant for the rest of our day. I would go to the hospital and get checked out. The rest of the tour group would continue without us. Olivia and Lily would wait in a boring foreign hospital while I was checked, and something was done to correct the heart rhythm. Such an awesome day together was ruined by me. At least it was only Friday, and we still had a full four days of fun left at the resort to make up for the disappointment. As I sat between the two girls, unable to focus, deep in my thoughts, and quietly suffering, the entertainment started.

A woman mime appeared in a period Victorian dress like a statue and painted head-to-toe in chalk white. As she very slowly worked her way around the room, periodically stopping and striking a statuesque pose, a musician came out with a guitar. The musician, a man in his late fifties or early sixties, went from table to table, serenading the guests. I had a hard time paying attention to anything, and I dreaded the thought of him coming over to our table. My daughters are two beautiful young ladies, so of course, he headed straight for us. He was a very good, talented musician, and when he arrived, I tried to give him as much attention as I could without being too dismissive. Sitting through his serenade at our table was personal torture. I felt self-conscious enough with everyone's eyes on me because of my blackout. Now, the attention was even more intense as this man continued to play his music. Once he was finished with his song, and before he could continue into another, I asked if he had a music CD to sell. Luckily, he produced one and placed it on the table.

I was sweating and silently suffering with my heart. I kindly asked Olivia if she could interact with a purchase. Whatever the cost of the CD, I was willing to pay. I just needed him to leave. The man said 3- peso, and I directed Olivia to go into my wallet and hand him a 5- peso bill. There was no way I wanted to get into any negotiations, and I told the musician to keep the change and thank you very much. Satisfied with the payment and acknowledgment, the man moved on.

I was very relieved and went back to sipping my beverage. I needed to give our tour guide, Rosemary, a heads-up on my decision to go to the hospital. I got up and walked over to her table, and I told her that once everyone finished their lunch, I would like to be taken to the hospital. Rosemary seemed relieved at my decision, reiterating that it was a large hospital and it was very close. Rosemary then stated that we would be finishing very soon, and then they would take us.

Sitting back down with Olivia and Lily, I told them that we were going to head straight to the hospital once everyone had finished their lunch. It was hard to make conversation as we were all pretty stressed out at the situation. Shortly, Rosemary approached our table and asked if I was able to drive to the hospital. I said that I didn't feel comfortable and that I would rather not. Pat arrived by our side before leaving and offered to drive our jeep. I was very thankful he initiated and offered to help. As we drove away from the restaurant, Pat tried to make a small supportive conversation, and I appreciated the gesture. I could hear sympathy in the tone of his voice. Going to a foreign hospital while on vacation is nobody's wish, and he knew it was a hard decision to make. I couldn't talk much during the drive as my thoughts were elsewhere, to the unknown future. I had no idea this day would be imprinted on me forever.

The drive only took about five minutes, and during that time, I was sweaty, nervous, and a bit frightened. We parked along the side of the road to the northeast of the hospital. The hospital, Hospital General Provincial Roberto Rodriguez Fernandez, was larger than I imagined. It consisted of three floors. The structure was yellow brick with burnt sienna trim. Architecturally, it was institutional, without character, and in complete contrast to the intricate historical homes and buildings that surrounded it. We got out of the jeep, and Olivia grabbed our backpack containing our meager possessions for that day. Rosemary waved to us to follow her to the entrance. I thanked Pat for his help, and he wished me luck as we left the group, heading towards the hospital. Where we had parked, there was an entrance, but we did not enter there. Later, I found out that the entrance was for employees only. Rosemary led the way along the northern end of the building with no visible doors or windows.

Rosemary was in a hurry to get into the hospital, and with Olivia and Lily in pursuit, I was being left behind. I was extremely slow and could not walk any faster as I was short of breath and fatigued. Walking around that building was like I was on the beach the day before, winded, tired, and just needing to sit and rest. I couldn't call out for them to wait for me as I didn't have the strength in my breath to do so. Eventually, Olivia and Lily stopped to look behind them to see how I was doing. To their surprise, I was far behind and waved to them, saying that I was okay but just couldn't walk as fast.

The building was large, and I had to set a goal for myself to make it to the corner, and then the entrance would be right there. Eventually, I reached the northwest corner and turned to see another 30 yards to the entrance. I then set another goal to get to the entrance without succumbing to my urge to sit down and rest. I thought to myself that it would be quite foolish to give up so close to the entrance of the hospital, and I kept going.

Rosemary and the girls waited at the front door of the hospital with me in sight. Once inside the hospital doors, Rosemary took off in a direction towards another group of doors with some seating on the other side. The entrance of the hospital led to a medium-sized lobby that did not have a reception desk or directory anywhere. There were some chairs set up in the front entrance of the hospital, like airport terminal seating, and that was all I could see. Thankfully, Rosemary was in charge and seemed to know where to go to get help. We followed her through a set of doors, and she said to wait there while she went to find help. The seating in the triage area was taken, so we found a wall for me to stand against while we waited. There were others standing as well, congregating around a doorway with louvered, slatted wooden doors. Every time a staff member from the hospital would go into the room, the small gathering would stretch to take a peek inside.

Standing in the waiting area, leaning against the wall for my rest and stability, Lily approached me and asked me how I was doing. I looked at her with a half-smile and shook my head, saying, "Not good, it still doesn't feel right." Lily and Olivia didn't know what to say and just stood with me in silence, waiting for Rosemary to return with someone who could help us.

After what seemed like an eternity, Rosemary approached, followed by a tall, thin, middle-aged woman dressed in hospital whites and carrying a clipboard. Rosemary was talking Spanish to the woman, filling her in on what had transpired before we had arrived at the hospital. Rosemary gestured to us to follow them. We went back through the front lobby of the hospital to a very small, dark cinder block walled room with a single bed and portable Electrocardiogram (ECG) machine. The room was too small for everyone to be in, so Olivia and Lily stood halfway through the doorway. The hospital lady could not speak English, so Rosemary translated for me, telling me to remove my shirt and lay down on the bed as they were going to record my heartbeat. An Electrocardiogram records the electrical function of the heart, which is also described as the rhythm of the heart over a certain period of time.

As I removed my shirt, I remember thinking how thankful I was that Rosemary was able to get me some attention and care so fast. Left to our own devices, I might have still been wandering around the hospital trying to find someone to talk to and explain my situation. The Electrocardiogram (ECG) machine had a number of leads coming from it, which had large suction cup ends to attach to my skin. The technician placed electrical clamps from the machine around both my ankles and wrists and the suctioning electrodes on my chest and sides. A number of the suction cup ends had a hard time suctioning to my skin and kept popping off. Every time a suction would pop off, I would have to get the attention of the technician in order to have it suctioned on my skin again. She didn't seem too perturbed at first, as if it was a usual occurrence. I had an ECG reading, and eventually, after a few tries, the ECG technician was able to properly attach all the wires to me. My heart was still palpitating. This was a good thing, as perhaps they could really have a go at figuring out what was going on.

I had gone to a hospital in the past with symptoms, and by the time I arrived at the hospital and was seen by a doctor, the symptoms that led me there had passed. In those instances, I felt a bit of a fool and also concerned I was not going to receive a proper, informed diagnosis. Being able to lie down was nice as it was the first time I was able to really relax since this situation started. I lay still on the small hospital bed and, as quietly as I could, let the ECG machine take its reading. I hoped they would catch something wrong and have a good, solid answer for me. I was looking forward to getting a diagnosis and a correction for my situation so we could get on with our day and enjoy the rest of our vacation.

While waiting for the results, I looked toward Olivia and Lily and gave them a reassuring smile. They both smiled back, but I knew they were worried and stressed. I was trying to keep emotionally strong for them, and they were doing the same in return.

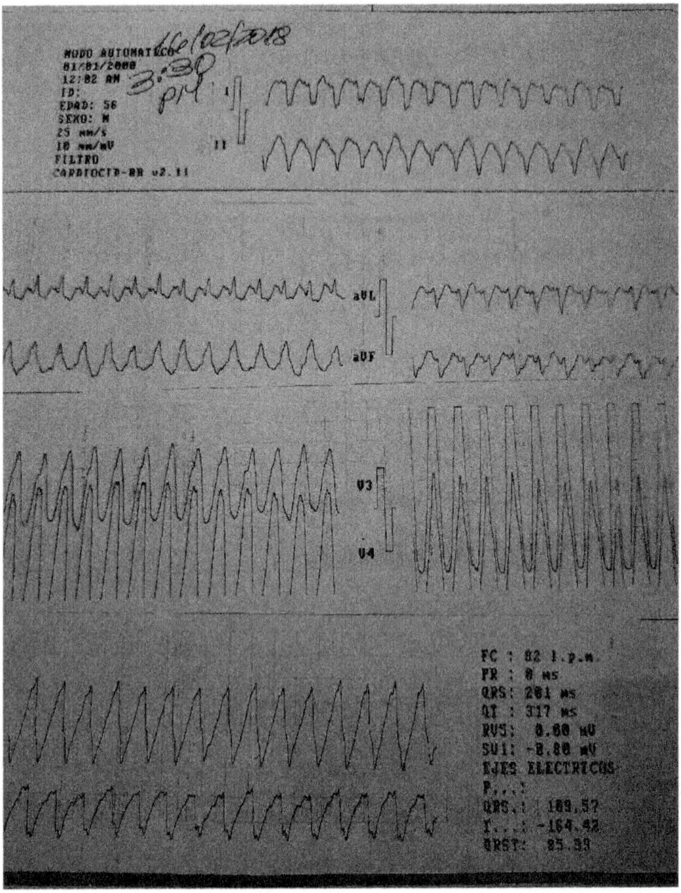

ECG upon entering Cuban hospital 3:30pm

A very short period of time later, the ECG machine started pumping out a reading of my heart rhythm. The ECG technician had deep wrinkles, wore heavy makeup, and had large dark-rimmed glasses. She had bright red lipstick accentuating thick lips, and her dark hair was pulled back into a tight ponytail. She did not speak English, and I could not speak or understand Spanish, so I was fixated on her facial expressions, searching for any sign to give me insight.

The technician tore the paper away from the machine and started analyzing the results. She looked down towards me, and her accentuated lips stretched out into a wide frown. Her head started to sway side to side in disappointment. There was an odd compassion to her look implying both, *you poor man, you don't have a chance* and *you're screwed.*

It was not the look I had hoped for, and it was the first time I really felt a deep sense of worry. My worry was no longer about ruining our day excursion or our family vacation anymore. My worry was about my health, what was really wrong with me, and whether I was going to survive. Can they really help me? The technician gestured towards Rosemary and started explaining the ECG results to her. Rosemary was listening intently and taking it all in. My fierce Spanish champion's face of concern crumbled and turned to compassionate disbelief. She was obviously a bit shaken and nervous. Slight panic could now be heard in her voice as she instructed me to put my shirt back on. Olivia and Lily sensed the same change in demeanor and started to stand straight and attentive, like they needed to do something to help.

As I sat up on the edge of the bed in that darkened cinder block room, Rosemary relayed what was going to happen next. She said that I must now go up to the foreigner's wing, where I will be admitted to the hospital. Rosemary then assured me that this area was for tourists and that it was nice. Rosemary asked me if I could stand up. I thought it was an unusual question as I had just walked almost halfway around the hospital and to the ECG room without any assistance. There was concern and caring in her voice that was new. Until then, she was very directive and abrupt in her communication, a good characteristic that someone who was in charge needed to possess.

As I stood up, she reached towards me as if to support me if I were to fall, but my situation had unfortunately changed since entering the room and laying on the bed. I felt lightheaded and a bit weak. I replied, "I think I shouldn't walk because I don't feel right, and I'm not sure how far I can go,"

Shortly after I indicated that I would need assistance getting to the foreigner's wing, a young, thin man with curly blond hair showed up outside the small doorway pushing a wheelchair. This young man was fully Caucasian, and his fashion choices were from the 1980s hair band era. He wore classic skinny jeans and a black Van Halen concert t-shirt. I wondered how long he was marooned stuck on this island. Did he wander away from friends at a concert and somehow, miraculously wash up on Cuba's shore?

Strange and nostalgic sight, but he was here to help, and I appreciated it. I sat in the wheelchair, and it felt unusual as I had never been in a wheelchair out of necessity before. Before we left, the technician handed Rosemary the ECG results in a file, and we parted ways. The young rocker dude pushed me through the hospital with Rosemary, Olivia, and Lily following closely.

Leaving the bright, sunlit front foyer of the main entrance, we went through a large set of glass and metal doors. We were now being led through the main inner hallways of the hospital. A couple dozen locals lined the walls on our way to the elevators to take us to the third floor. Every eye was on me as we passed by. I felt like the new kid on his first day of school. It must have been a sight: A middle-aged white guy being wheeled through the Cuban hospital's hallway pushed by a skinny, white head banger and followed by an entourage of young women trying to keep up.

There was little to no lighting throughout the hospital passageway's inner structure. Institutional construction consisting of exposed cement and large brown tinted tile lined this hospital. The only light enabling us to see came from an open-air vestibule of greenery cutting into the center of the building, reaching three stories to the sunny skies above. The sunlight did not make it to the far corners, creating dark shadows and dead spaces.

I was wheeled to an elevator with Rosemary close behind, holding the results of the ECG close to her chest. The elevator was not only slow but made heavy clanging noises of metal against metal. The elevator box sounded like it was hitting the walls of the shaft like a tilt-a-whirl at an amusement park. The elevator door opened with a long, drawn-out squeak. An older man was sitting on a chair inside the elevator, not doing much other than supervising the coming and going of people in the elevator. He definitely was not the concierge-type who asked which floor you wanted to go to. He looked like he had been trapped there for decades, riding up and down with no emotion left in him, not even enough to make eye contact or smile. I made an assumption that this was the Communist government's way of employing elderly people, making them sit on elevators all day and making sure people didn't take the elevator for joy rides or dares.

The elevator took us up to the top floor, exiting us to the still-darkened hospital corridors. A quick turn to the left was the frosted glass and stainless-steel entrance to the tourist wing. Opening and proceeding through the doors was like entering into a completely new, modern building. The walls changed from drab and shadowy cement with brown veined tile to white drywall with painted accents of pale blues and greens. The floor was a clean white marble with moldings running the length of the hallways on each side.

Eventually, we came upon an actual nurse's reception area with nurses dressed in white uniforms with the iconic white nurse's cap. I gave a huge sigh of relief at the sight of the space I just entered. It was welcoming compared to what we had traveled through to get here. We were ushered into a room opposite the nurse's station.

The room was light, with windows along the far wall. A small couch sat to the right of the door, followed by a bed that doubled as an examination table. Opposite the couch and bed was a large bathroom. I was instructed to leave the wheelchair and sit on the examination bed. Olivia and Lily took a seat on the couch, with Lily closest to me, and Rosemary stood close by them next to the doorway.

Three nurses simultaneously walked into the room, and Rosemary handed the ECG results to one of them. Rosemary, who I suppose was the head nurse, conversed in Spanish together about the events leading up to now. Two other nurses gathered around me as I sat on the side of the bed, thinking about my heart and wondering when someone was going to do something to physically help me.

The head nurse gently approached me and proceeded to ask me how I was feeling. I began to describe the palpitations that I had been having over the past couple of hours and how I had blacked out in the car. I didn't go into speculating about my past anxiety attacks and irregular heartbeat that I was diagnosed with years ago. I wanted to be precise and factual about what was happening to me at that moment. I felt that whatever I was going through was completely new to me, something that I had not experienced before.

Friday 7 p.m., Foaming Bubbles

The room was very calm and a bit surreal to me, as there didn't seem to be any sense of urgency. I was suffering physically with a heart that wasn't beating properly, mentally anxious and stressed out, not knowing what was wrong. After describing my circumstances, I suddenly felt really sick to my stomach. The stress and anxiety I had been feeling over the past couple hours was finally getting to me, and whatever small amount was in my stomach at the time was not staying there. I jumped out of my sitting position on the bed and bounded towards the bathroom opposite the couch where Olivia and Lily were sitting. Halfway to the toilet bowl was the best I could do. Luckily, I only drank the lime soda and had nothing else to eat. Thinking I was finished, I tried to head back to the side of the bed but only returned halfway. I felt embarrassed knowing that someone else would have to clean up after my mess. After a couple of attempts to regain control of my reflux, I was able to return to the bed, continually apologizing to the nurses for not being able to restrain my stomach. I sat back down on the side of the bed feeling defeated but also a bit more relaxed as the knot in my stomach was gone.

Suddenly, I began feeling lightheaded, similar to when I was driving in the jeep before I blacked out, and my breathing became shallower and weaker. Lily was right beside the bed, sitting on the couch. She leaned over towards me to say something, looked up at me with her already big, beautiful eyes, even more widened with concern, and with an optimistic tone, asked me, "Are you feeling better now?"

The question made me smile inside. Turning to Lily while still sitting on the hospital bed, I tried to smile through my worry, saying, "No, not really."

Not knowing what situation lay before me, I never thought that I wouldn't see them again. I had imagined my death much differently, where the family would be gathered around my aged, frail body. I would have the chance to tell them that I loved them and that I had a good and meaningful long life. I would tell my wife and children that I loved them very much, very deeply. I knew Louise, and I had given them love and the best opportunity to succeed in life as we could. I knew I instilled a good foundation of faith in God that they could explore. Olivia and Lily would grow with their own families, careers, and responsibilities. Had I known what my future held for me a mere five minutes in advance, I wouldn't ever have let them leave that room without saying goodbye.

A couple of doctors entered and quickly spoke to one of the nurses. That nurse then turned to Rosemary and my kids and told them that it was time for them to leave. The doctors approached me, and behind them, I could see my children being escorted out of the room. I had a mere second to make eye contact with them as they disappeared through the doorway and into the hallway.

My focus was directed to the two doctors before me. I saw a strong and well-built young black doctor accompanied by a much older and lighter-skinned doctor with graying military-style buzz-cut hair and dark-rimmed glasses. The young black doctor introduced himself as Dr. Rodriguez. "So, I was told you are having heart palpitations. Can you tell me what happened and how you are feeling now?"

I relayed what had happened, starting with the heart palpitations and all that started happening a couple of hours ago.

The doctor asked, "Are you still having the palpitations?"

I said that the palpitations were still happening and that it felt like butterflies in my chest.

"Okay, I need you to lay down so we can examine you," Dr. Rodriguez turned to the other doctor to converse. Meanwhile, a couple of the nurses stepped closer to me and started taking off my sandals, watch, glasses, and wedding ring. I swung my legs onto the bed and laid back, resting on a slight incline. The two doctors and nurses surrounded the bed. Dr. Rodriguez grasped my right wrist and pressed deeply, checking for my pulse while the other doctor and nurses stared down at me, silhouetted by the ceiling-height rectangular windows behind them. The doctors and nurses were talking in Spanish, and at that moment, my situation drastically changed.

Laying back on the examination bed in an inclined position, my breathing became very labored and short. My chest rose up quickly with little gasps of air as I felt oxygen tubes being placed around my cheeks and into my nostrils. I thought, *At least the oxygen will help, and they are being more proactive with my condition.* This new development of being unable to get oxygen was frightening. I don't know what to do. I felt helpless. I had a large audience of medical professionals surrounding me. *They must be able to do something for me!*

I looked up towards the doctors and nurses while Dr. Rodriguez still had a strong hold on my wrist. The pressure was starting to fade, but not because he was letting go. I began losing the sensation of physical touch beginning with the extremities of my hands and feet, rapidly moving upwards toward the middle of my body; I lost awareness of my body. I had no feeling.

It was like my nervous system just shut down. My gasping for air stopped.

My chest was not heaving up and down. It was still. With stillness now enveloping me, the room became increasingly quiet. The doctor's voice muffled like heavily padded stereo headphones were placed over my ears. All the sounds surrounding me fade to silence. I thought my eyes were playing a trick on me. My sight of the medical professionals blurred. I was losing the ability to make out their facial features, like I had just taken off prescription glasses, and their features all blended together.

But behind the blurry silhouettes, light was beginning to fill the room. The ceiling-high windows allowed the sunny afternoon light in, but the light surrounding everyone was not coming from outside. The light was glowing from inside the examination room. It filled the room with a pure, nontransparent aura of white light that was foreign and new. I knew I was dying. I was losing this battle for life and had no way of fighting for it. I could not take back control. I must accept my situation for what it is. I had no choice. My last day on this earth was at age 46. Absent from my family and with people I had never met. They only know me as some poor, unfortunate tourist.

The room was quickly filling with bright white light. It swallowed everyone and everything in the room. It made everything disappear. I was in a sea of light. Now, completely conscious and aware, I was in complete white.

After losing all physical notions of my body, I had only one physical sensation left, and that was off my lips. I could feel foaming bubbles coming up through my lips and popping like I did when drinking milk as a kid. I had no idea why this happened, and I tried to understand why the bubbles were forming.

I am fully aware, and never having lost consciousness, I was afraid but surprisingly calm. Through the bubbles forming in my mouth, I am able to use the breath that was left in me to say two words, "Jesus, Jesus."

I wanted to keep repeating His name a third time, but halfway through His name, my breath was gone. Extinguished. It was in my last couple of seconds and in my last expenditure of breath that I called out to Him for help.

Now, I was completely disengaged from my body and completely separated from my surroundings. I only heard my own thoughts and had no physical feelings. The sensation of breathing, the rise and fall of my chest, no longer existed. There was no bodily sensation and no longer an awareness of what was once around me in the physical realm of the hospital. I remained calm and very peaceful.

My consciousness remained suspended in the surrounding white just long enough for me to accept that I had no control over what was happening to me and no control over what was going to happen next. I still feel that I had the chance to go back to the examination room and that the doctors will do something to bring me back. I had not given up hope that they would intervene in some way: give me an injection, hook me up to a medical device, perform CPR. Anything. Still being conscious, I feel I am somehow still physically alive and had hope that things would go back to normal. By whatever medical miracle, I still hung onto the idea that the process of this experience would somehow reverse itself. *There will be a rational explanation of why I do not have any sensation of my surroundings, and I will say thank you for your help and continue on my way back to the resort with Olivia and Lily.*

I began to feel as though I was being pulled. Not a physical pull by someone's hand, but a gravitational one like what an object would feel being sucked into a vacuum. Our bodies are merely a vehicle to house our souls while on our earthly journey. I had died and did not have any use for it anymore. My soul separated from my body. The separation did not hurt and was rather comical with a slight "pop" sensation. It released like being shot out of a cannon, offering unencumbered freedom of movement.

I immediately felt a weightlessness and moved rapidly away from my body. I was traveling, as I could still feel the gravitational pull. I was in completely different surroundings. It was now dark but not pitch black. I could see color and what seemed like far away stars around me as I traveled. Very calm and matter of fact, I said to myself, *Well, I guess I just died. I wonder what's going to happen next?*

I had no control over what was happening to me, and I had immediate acceptance that it was time for me to move on and accept whatever adventure awaited me.

Suddenly, my soul stopped moving. Although I was at the mercy of whatever was coming up next, I felt relaxed and at peace. I found myself looking down upon the earth. It was quiet, the earth suspended in space, the darkness of space surrounding it. As I was looking at the earth, I thought of Louise and was immediately in her presence. I could see her driving along a road close to our home —a route she would normally take to go shopping or run errands. I was with her for only a few seconds and felt that she was going to be okay. I didn't know what was in her future, but I knew it would be a struggle for her to raise our two daughters by herself. She would be strong and move along through life without me. The thought of her being alright without me didn't upset me. Knowing that she would be okay was like closing a chapter in my life, and it gave me inner peace and permission to continue on my journey.

After having that feeling of closure, I was once again above the earth, looking down on this huge, beautiful marble floating in space. I thought of my children and knew that they would have a difficult time with my passing. The thought of them without me bothered me, but I didn't know what to do about it. I don't know how to change the situation I was in. With regret, I had to accept and move on. The earth then shot into the distance, getting smaller with incredible speed, and within what seemed to be a split second, it disappeared.

Chapter closed. My life on earth was no more.

Instantly, I was in a seamless transition back to my consciousness in the white light that surrounded me in the hospital—after I fearfully called out to Jesus through the bubbles between my lips.

The surroundings started to change color to a golden hue. Gradually, it started to move, and I could see clouds forming around me.

Quickly, I found myself surrounded by billowing golden clouds, and I felt incredible peace. It was a peace so strong and comforting, and it was like nothing I had ever experienced before. I didn't know the peace I was experiencing could ever exist. Floating in the golden clouds, I was thinking to myself, *after everything I just went through, the palpitations, the hospital, the stress around not knowing what was happening to me, the thought of me dying, how can I be so relaxed and feeling such peace and no worry?*

I was afraid when I was having trouble breathing and when I called out to Jesus. Now, floating amongst the golden clouds, I had no more fear. Fear did not exist in me at all. I knew I had died and moved on into another realm because my surroundings were so different and so profoundly real. This type of surrounding and experience simply did not exist in my life on earth. I had no connection with my body as it no longer existed.

The bubbles that were between my lips had long disappeared right after my last two words of "Jesus." The physical ability of speech through the anatomy of vocal cords, breath, and lips also no longer existed. I was a soul, consciousness, and without a body. I felt as if I existed as energy and did not possess the physical ability to speak. I had never seen golden clouds like these before and was in awe of their beauty. The clouds were small, slightly transparent, and moved quickly like billowing smoke in a room. I felt confined. I was not able to move, and the golden clouds were like a veil, keeping me from seeing anything too far beyond. There was no odor, no sound, no physical feeling of touch or temperature, just my soul floating among this beautiful phenomenon.

But I was also not alone.

The most perfect of days with my daughters had taken a drastic turn, and I succumbed to the idea I died. I knew I was dead. It wasn't like falling asleep and finding myself in a dream. I never once lost consciousness and was fully aware throughout the entire experience. Whatever I expected the doctors and nurses to do to help my situation did not come to fruition. I accepted I had died, and I was in awe of my surroundings and in wonder of what was going to come next. It was the most amazing adventure, and I looked forward to learning more about what life was going to be after death.

As the golden clouds continued to move around me, I saw something move. I focused on the movement, and a beautiful orb of color goes from my right and glides left. I immediately knew that it was a being, my guardian angel. It was behind the clouds, but the colors that made up its form were radiating and shone through. It was energy in an oval shape with pointed ends at the top and bottom. It did not have a distinct outline, but light emitting from it was formed and protruded a short distance from the center.

As this light entity slowly and gracefully moved from one side of my vision to the other, its center pulsated auras of purple, blue, white, and a strange silver color like liquid mercury. The colors were radiant and swirled around the center energy like a rolling marble. I felt comforted knowing that someone was with me. I knew it had been with me, knew me, and it was there for me. I marveled at its beautiful array of moving colors. It was impolite to just stare, so I naturally greeted the other soul by thinking, "Hello, aren't you beautiful?" in a friendly voice. The soul continued on its path, faded, and disappeared behind the clouds. Disappointed but not fearful, I was on my own, not knowing what to expect next.

I did not know how to look around at my surroundings. I did not have a body with muscle mobility to manipulate the direction of my vision, so whatever was in front of me at the time was all I could see. I was now floating, suspended, in a sea of comfort and peace. Not knowing how my line of sight moved away from the clouds, and I was able to look out into space with countless stars in the distance.

No longer was I in awe of my surroundings as I was enveloped with the emotion that surrounded and permeated every inch of my soul. The peace I felt was indescribable. It was tangible and had a physicality to it that could be felt with incredible intensity throughout my entire entity and radiating around me. The feeling was overwhelming and euphoric. I had never felt so peaceful in my life, and it felt amazing.

No worries, no deadlines, no commitments, and no troubles looming in the back of my mind. My soul was completely free from all worldly constraints, habits, and vices. My moments of euphoria on earth, where I would feel "light as a feather," good about myself, relaxed, and thankful, would only last for a few seconds the excitement, wonder, and relaxed happiness would leave as quickly as it came. Where I was in life after death, the peaceful euphoria did not dissipate over time. The peaceful emotion was constant and continuously building. I closed my vision to concentrate on the incredible feeling and take it all in.

As I opened myself to sight, I was looking out into an abyss of stars reflecting off a glass-like plane with a distant horizon. Still feeling the peace, I said to myself, *how long will this feeling last?* Just as I rhetorically asked myself that question, my mind's vision rapidly shot out through space along this plane. I traveled with great velocity creating a tunnel vision with stars, space, and majestic colors of red, blue, and purple passed by. It felt like I could have gone on for eternity with nothing impeding me. I traveled through this tunnel with such rapid acceleration that I started to feel uncomfortable at how far I had gone within a few seconds.

As soon as I felt apprehension, I was immediately back to where I had started and found myself amongst the golden clouds again. I thought to myself, *Wow, that was crazy!* I knew that I had just experienced eternity, as I could have gone on forever with only the command of a thought.

I asked a question: *How long is this feeling of peace going to last?*

Eternity, was the instantaneous answer!

I was once again floating in the golden clouds and wondering what was going to be the next step of my journey. I am living quite the adventure, traveling by thought, discovering and learning new things. I don't have any fear as I felt very much alive, so I want to keep moving forward. I was eager to discover what was in store for me. I still could not move my vision around freely as I didn't know how to without a neck.

A bright white, radiating light started to appear in the lower right of my field of vision. A light so intense that it dissipated the golden clouds and flooded my vision with pure white surroundings. This light was much different than the white light that surrounded me on the hospital examination table.

This approaching light was radiating emotion.

When people make statements about going towards the "light" and seeing the "light" at the end of the tunnel, the "light" is not like a light bulb. I could feel this "light" hitting me, permeating me, flowing through me, and touching every part of my soul. It was love! It was radiating love that sent warm shivers and vibrations through me.

The love was so powerful and intense that I instantly knew it was God.

The clouds completely disappeared because of the intensity of the radiating love, and I was once again in a sea of white. But this sea of white was charged with pure love.

I started being pulled towards the source of the love. I knew I was moving. I could feel the pull, and I could feel my soul rolling around in love like a slow, uncontrolled fall. The feeling of love, as I was being drawn closer to God, kept building in intensity. I knew I was rapidly on my way to heaven and eventually going to be face to face with God and my judgment. My demeanor became more serious as the finality of my death became more apparent the closer I approached God. Until this time, everything had been rather fun, full of positive emotion, floating in that emotion like a jellyfish riding the ocean tides.

As I was getting closer to God, I started to think about my mortality and felt it wasn't my time. I hadn't met God yet and knew He would be the one who would ultimately decide my fate. I had not been judged, and I had not entered into what I believed to be heaven. Knowing that I held onto the idea that this adventure of life after death was only temporary and that I could somehow still recover and end up back in the Cuban hospital. There was a chance that the doctors were working on me and still trying to find a solution to bring me back. I had no idea how; my fate was no longer up to me. The more I traveled, the closer I got to God; I knew I needed to speak. I had to attempt to convey how I felt; I still had things to do, and it seemed too early in my life to be moving on.

As my soul was being drawn closer to the light and radiant love of God, I felt the need to plead my case because it was not my time. I still had some hope that it was not too late to return to earth. My only hand to deal with was I still needed to get baptized. It was already arranged at our new church on my next birthday along with Lily. But it hadn't happened yet. Although this was an emotionally beautiful place, I still felt I had more life to live on earth. I guess I was just having a hard time accepting what had happened. It was such a beautiful day with my daughters, and thinking that it was one of the best days we had ever had together, my death didn't seem legit.

I tried to speak but was unable. I no longer had a physical body to create and project a voice. For a moment, I was a bit stumped as to how to communicate. All I could do to communicate was to pray. I had prayed most of my life. Surely, if I were to pray silently in my mind, He would hear me.

I started to plead, *Heavenly Father, it's not my time. It can't be my time. I'm not even baptized yet. I'm supposed to be baptized next month on the eighteenth!*

There was no response. Although I had yet to be baptized, it was not a concern or requirement to receive God's love. In fact, after I had made that seemingly pathetic plea of baptism, I continued to be pulled towards the light, God's love, even faster. I tried to look around, but all I could see was that I was still completely surrounded by bright, pure white. The white around me had no shadows, no flaws, and its intensity was powerful. The love radiating around and through me from Him was gaining intensity, and it literally started to make me laugh with joy and pleasure. I knew that if this feeling of love were to continue to get more and more intense, it would get harder and harder for me to want to leave and return to earth.

I was on the cusp of giving into His powerful love and accepting my fate when I was telepathically asked a question, "Which way would you like to go?"

Telepathy is a concept that I was aware of but obviously had never before experienced. There was no sound of voice but rather a thought placed amongst my own thoughts that I did not create. Confused, not understanding if I had manifested that question or if it come from someone else, I asked myself, "was that my thinking, or was that someone else asking me a question?" As I asked that of myself, I was interrupted by, "Which way would you like to go?" I realized by own rationalizing thought was completely interrupted, and I was again asked the same question. Right away, I knew it was not my own thoughts swirling around in my mind, but God's communication with me, asking me a question and allowing me a choice in my fate.

From the time I had left my body in the examination room until now, I was having a pretty good time. I was feeling some incredibly amazing emotions of peace and love, and I had witnessed a few fantastic sights that were in keeping with many images of our universe's deep space.

I was now given a choice. I could continue on towards God and His love or revert back to the physical realm of earth. Pain, sorrow, worry, financial, work, and family stress awaited me if I were to decide to return. Life with God was looking pretty good to me. I knew I needed to answer God.

My demeanor became serious as I knew it was time to make one of the most important decisions of my existence. I didn't want Him to have to ask a third time. There was a strong awareness that it was just Him and I. I felt connected to Him, and all His attention was on me. Of all the other things going on at that moment on earth, with billions of lives throughout the universe and beyond, God was with me and only me. I was all that mattered at that moment, or so I thought.

Before I could answer His question, God showed me my daughters. I had been so wrapped up in what was happening to me, taking in every amazing moment of my death, looking forward to what was to come, I had forgotten about my responsibility as a father. I assumed my death was final and there was nothing I could do about it. I had to trust that everyone was going to be okay, looked after, and move on. A vision appeared before me. God allowed me to see Olivia and Lily in the hospital room beside the room my body was in. Olivia was standing up and had a cell phone in her hand, and Lily was sitting on a blue chair next to her and looking up at her. They both looked concerned and worried and were all alone. I was looking down upon them, but I was not actually in the room with them. They were like a vision, and I was watching them through a screen.

They were alone in Cuba without me. They were frightened and did not know what to do. I wanted to be with them.

I knew they still very much needed me in their lives, especially now. Given the choice, there was no way I could leave them. I was their dad, their protector, and they were my responsibility. I loved them, and they needed me to be with them more than ever.

My mind settled, and I knew what I needed to do. I prayed. Throughout my life, I struggled to translate thoughts into words. Very often, I would say the wrong thing at an inappropriate time or have it come out wrong. Emotions would intertwine with my communication, and I would have trouble getting to the point.

In the presence of God, my thoughts were clear, precise, and to the point. I noticed right away that I did not have any trouble saying what I needed and wanted to say.

I prayed, "Heavenly Father, if it is my time and you need me, then I am willing to go. But, if it is not my time and you don't really need me, then I need to stay. My girls are in a foreign country all alone, and they need me, and I need to be with them!"

Friday, Time Unknown: The Return

As soon as I finished my final word, I was instantly back in my body. I immediately opened my eyes. The first physical sensation I had was a regular and steady heartbeat. I felt my heartbeat through my chest. I can almost hear it pumping. It was steady without flaw. The palpitations were gone. The healthy heartbeat was God's way of showing me that I was going to be okay. I was back. God stayed true to my choice. I felt at ease and was hopeful that my life would resume back to the wonderful time I was having with Olivia and Lily. I was hopeful to leave the hospital, go back to the resort, and enjoy the rest of our trip.

To my surprise, slowly looking around the room, the room was empty of everyone except one nurse who was at the foot of my bed. She didn't notice I was back, conscious, and very much alive. She was not paying any attention other than standing there looking around like she was waiting for a bus at a bus stop. I noticed the room was much darker than I remembered before going on my spiritual journey. Time did pass on earth, but I do not know how much time. The doctors and nurses who were enveloped in white light, surrounding my bed, and supposed to be fighting for my life had disappeared.

I wondered how long I was gone but then realized that the lights had been turned off. Daylight was still coming through the windows, but it was more subdued, like the light of early evening. The once bright, sun-filled room was now shades of grey. There was a metal gurney beside the bed with a thin top mattress that wasn't there before. I also had an IV drip inserted into my left arm. *Where did all the doctors go?* Last time I remembered this room, it was filled with nurses and doctors surrounding my bed, looking for a pulse and placing oxygen tubes in my nose.

Oxygen tubes are gone, doctors gone, lights out, and nurses—except one who was not paying attention to me—are all gone!

I shifted to face the nurse at the end of the bed. I startled her. She gives a slight jerk in her body to face me. Our eyes meet. Her eyes go wide at the sight of me awake. I raised my right arm and gently waved at her, and said the only Spanish greeting I know, "Hola."

The nurse, with a strained tone in her voice like she wasn't prepared to speak, returned a raspy, "Hola."

I smiled at her, and slowly, her eyes and mouth simultaneously widened into a beautiful expression of happiness. She immediately turned her attention toward the open door of the examination room and tried to get the attention of some people outside the door.

I prop myself up onto my elbows for a better look around the room. The nurse, seeing I was alive, well, and starting to get up to sit on the side of the bed, motions frantically and shouts at the people in the hallway to come into the room. Concerned about me moving around, the nurse said, "No, no, we do, we do." A couple of men, orderlies, come rushing into the room. The nurse does not want me to move off the bed and tells me to lie back down. Feeling fully capable of rising off the bed and transferring myself to the gurney, I keep gesturing for me to move myself. The nurse insisted, "No, no, no, we do, we do."

The orderlies rush to the head and foot of the bed. I figure I might as well comply and not ruffle anyone's feathers. I do not want to get anyone in trouble for not doing what they were supposed to do. I laid back down on the examination bed. The orderlies wrapped the ends of the sheets in their hands and proceeded to lift me to the gurney.

I was immediately wheeled out of the room and turned right down the hallway towards the glass wall and doors that I had entered through to the foreigner's wing. I was taken back to the only elevator that serviced the north side of the hospital. The elevator was not very large, and not everyone could fit. The head of my gurney was right up against the back wall, the elevator supervisor sat in the corner on a stool, still reluctant to make eye contact with anyone, and one orderly came into the elevator as well. The doors began to close. A loud echoing "bang" rang through the elevator shaft and hallway. The gurney jolted sideways. It was too long for the elevator. The situation caught everyone by surprise, especially me. Before anyone could react, the door slammed into the gurney again, and a little heated conversation broke out between the orderlies.

I found the situation to be quite funny and began to quietly laugh in disbelief while shaking my head. Eventually, they figure out they need to take the foot barrier of the bed off in order for it to fit into the elevator. Once disassembled, the elevator door was able to close, and only one orderly was able to accompany me down to the first floor while the other orderly ran down two stories of stairs to meet us.

Once on the first floor, I was wheeled back towards the entrance of the hospital and ended up going back through the red doors of the triage area where Olivia, Lily, and I had waited for Rosemary to find help only hours earlier.

I was quite the spectacle for the locals standing in the hallways. The triage area behind the red louvered saloon doors was a small space. There was only enough room for about four to five beds and only three partitioned areas. I was taken to the first partitioned area immediately to the right of the red doors and was positioned comfortably with a heart rate monitor clamped around my finger. I paid attention to my heart rate, and it was still a normal steady beat. Knowing that my heart was beating normally and I felt fine, I was hoping this would all be cleared up quickly. I would collect my daughters and head back to the resort to continue our vacation.

Before the orderlies left, I was told that someone would be with me shortly and that I would be waiting for a cardiologist to ultrasound my heart. The examination area is very small, with only enough room for one person on either side of the gurney. I was left alone as I waited.

Not able to get up and move around, I have a look around the room. The ceiling tiles are badly stained from water damage, and some are broken, and some missing. As I looked to my sides towards the green walls, I saw blood stains splattered up the sides. *What the heck happened in here, and why would they not clean up?*

Meanwhile, visitors to the hospital who were waiting and wondering how their loved ones were doing kept swinging the red doors open and quickly peeking into the room. I was constantly looking down past my feet towards the door and smiling at the onlookers. If they looked in long enough, I eventually waved to them and smiled. I waited a long time before anyone came to check on me. A male nurse eventually came into my partitioned space with a new IV bag to replace the saline solution they had given me for dehydration.

He explains, "This is a medicine called Amiodarone. Amiodarone is an anti-arrhythmic medication to treat serious irregular heartbeats. It restores the heart to a regular rhythm and blocks certain electrical currents to the heart that cause irregular heartbeats."

Just what I needed, although a bit too late! I thought. I did not want to take the chance of my heart acting up again, so I was thankful they had it available.

I waited quite a while in the blood-walled triage, with the locals looking in the room for their loved ones when a nurse finally came down from the foreigner's wing to visit me. She is a lovely, kind woman with a hospital administrator badge and introduced herself as the person looking after Olivia and Lily. She said, "They are doing well, being well looked after, very lovely and well mannered."

I replied, "Thank you for updating me. When may I see them?"

She produced her phone, saying, "They have recorded a short video of them for you."

Olivia and Lily were sitting on a couch in the room that I saw them in while in the presence of God. They each took a turn to say they were doing well, everyone was really nice, and they were being looked after. They said that they loved me and they hoped I'd be ok and feeling better.

The young administrator nurse then suggested I make a recording of myself on her phone to relay back to them. I assured them I was doing ok, "I'm feeling much better. I need to stay for some more tests. I love you both very much, and hopefully, we can see each other very soon."

The nurse administrator stopped the video, and I thanked her. She said,

"You will be going to the ICU after the ultrasound. Perhaps you can see them then."

As she left with the cell phone message to go back up to my daughters, I felt a sinking feeling inside. I was hoping to get out of the hospital as soon as possible. I was thinking after the cardiologist, seeing that my heart was back to normal, I could gather up Olivia and Lily and be done with this hospital nonsense.

Talking about me being admitted to the ICU was a devastating thought. I decided it was my number one priority to behave and act absolutely as normal as possible. I want to portray the vision of perfect health so they would have no reason to keep me. Albeit a bit shaken by what I had just gone through, I seemed fine and back to normal. I was very reluctant to let on that I knew I had died. I believed if I mentioned it, the conversation would get much more serious. I would have to admit that I knew how serious my condition was, and I wouldn't stand the chance to plead my case for release from the hospital. The hospital administration had everything of mine. My wallet, watch, shoes, passport, and money; the only possessions I had with me were the clothes on my back. My daughters were in their care somewhere in the hospital. I was at their mercy and needed to win the situation over with good behavior and good enough health to be released.

Friday: 8 p.m., the ICU

The cardiologist arrived right after some orderlies brought in ultrasound equipment. The area I was in was so small that they had trouble getting the equipment into the room next to me. They had to move my bed as far over to one side as possible. The cardiologist, a woman in her mid to late 40s, introduced herself in English which was better than most of the staff I had already encountered. What little she did speak, it was in medical terminology. I tried making small talk and warmed up to her, but she is not a conversationalist, doesn't make eye contact, and stays on task.

At the conclusion of the ultrasound, she tells me, "One of your ventricles, going to the left atrium, is not closing properly, and blood is being allowed to backflow. This condition may have contributed to low or disrupted blood pressure."

After blacking out in the vehicle, this makes sense to me.

She continues, "You will possibly need a valve replacement."

My heart jumped a little at the notion of heart surgery. *There is no way in hell I am going to allow a complicated valve replacement surgery to happen in this hospital or in this country,* I thought. *I know the Cuban doctors are well trained abroad, but the facilities and medical equipment from forty to fifty years ago just do not cut it. The recovery time after such a surgery would be long, and I have a plane to catch in less than five days!*

I thought about my girls again and could not help wondering what was going through their minds, and Louise at home worried, not knowing what was going on and being so far away from her family. I wished and hoped she would come down and be with

Olivia and Lily. I did not like being separated from the girls worrying on their own. The thought of them without their parents, in this situation, not knowing if I was going to live or die, is unbearable.

The cardiologist, after wrapping up her examination, said to me, "There is nothing we can do about it here; we don't do that type of surgery. Your situation is something you will need to get checked out when you get home."

I was so relieved to hear the surgery was not an option. I could get a second opinion when I got home. I don't need to make a life-or-death decision right now in a Cubin hospital. *I can buy some time to make such a big decision and get expert advice when I get home.*

Soon after the cardiologist left the triage area, the nurse administrator came into the room with two orderlies. She said, "We are heading to the ICU where you will recover."

Considering I was feeling pretty good, I was still hoping to get out and back to the resort by the next day. I knew it must have been getting late, so keeping me overnight for observation was acceptable. Once I proved my health was back to normal, they could send us back to our vacation. I would make it a priority to just relax, rest, and enjoy the pool, beach, and hospitality of the resort.

Before we left the triage area for the ICU, I asked, "How long am I going to have to stay in the ICU?"

I didn't want to have my hopes of leaving crushed. The nurse gave me a sympathetic smile and relayed my sentence, "You will be at least two to three days in the ICU."

My disappointed demeanor must have shown as she assured me that my daughters were being well cared for and stated that perhaps I could see them soon.

The gurney still had the end of it taken off, so it fit nicely and snugly into the elevator up to the second floor. I need to transfer onto another more comfortable ICU bed that I would stay in for the remainder of my recovery. I was again lifted from one to the other by a couple of orderlies grabbing the sheets underneath me at either end and lifting me to the new bed. I was wheeled down a long hallway to the last of two rooms that made up the ICU. Outside of the two ICU rooms was a desk that was a nurse's station. There were large windows looking into the ICU rooms from the desk. Upon entering my room, I noticed it was large enough for three beds and another nurse's desk. Windows were along the far wall. I could still see some daylight out the windows where there were trees and greenery, but the light was dull as the sun was setting. It was close to evening.

I thought of my girls. By the approximation of the sun, we must have been apart for quite some time now; hours have passed. My bed was directed to the far-right corner of the room up against the windows. I could not fully see out of the windows—they are much higher than the bed. A cinderblock wall sat beside me, and the windows merely gave me a slight glimmer of hope of again, one day, being outside in the fresh Caribbean air.

I have two ICU roommates. Directly across from me is an elderly lady with darkly tanned skin and deep wrinkles. Hard to tell as her skin is very weathered; she looks as though she is closing in on a century. Her eyes were shut, and she was not alert. I was not sure she knew I had entered the room. To my left, my neighbor is a young lady not much older than my eldest daughter, Olivia. The young lady was alert, aware, and seemed curious to see a pale-skinned, white guy from the cold north without any sun to darken his skin for months. I was the outcast of the group. Just as the young lady was looking at me, I, too, was wondering why someone so young was there. We traded glances and smiled at one another.

After the orderlies left, the doctor who first introduced himself to me in the examination room before I died, Dr. Rodriguez, entered the room. He was followed by a number of other young doctors. I was told the hospital is a teaching hospital, and there were a number of student doctors accompanying the resident doctors on their rounds.

Dr. Rodrigues introduced himself again by asking, "Do you remember me?"

I responded with a smile and a bit of a laugh because, to me, it was not that long ago.

"Yes, of course, how are you?" I replied.

Returning with a big smile. "I'm good," he said. "You are a lucky man, a very, very lucky man. We almost had to defibrillate you. We were very close to defibrillating!"

I always try to give someone the benefit of the doubt, but I think to myself, *that must be why the doctors were not in the examination room after I returned to my body. Perhaps they were off trying to find a defibrillator.* The state of the medical equipment I had seen was ancient in comparison to the standard in Canada. *Perhaps they have a limited number of defibrillators and had trouble finding one. If they had to rely on the elevators in that hospital, they would have never gotten to me in time, regardless,* I thought. Thinking back to my return, it still did not make sense to me that the medical staff left and the lights were turned off. I must have been there for quite some time. The oxygen that was initially in my nose had been removed, and there were no oxygen tanks to be seen. The gurney had, at some point, been wheeled in. I knew how much trouble they had getting it in the elevator, *so how much trouble and time did it take to get to my room?* I did have an IV in my arm with saline solution for hydration. I had heard stories of Air Ambulance services from Canada being called to retrieve patients from the Caribbean Islands, and upon arrival, the patients were already deceased. It was determined that IVs had been inserted post-mortem in order to collect more money from the insurance company.

I knew the medical team did not do anything for me. The fact I woke up alone and in a dark and abandoned room did not sit well with me. I did not ask questions of the doctor, and I did not want to let on that I knew they didn't do everything to save my life.

I felt uneasy. I didn't trust their medical judgment. I didn't feel safe in their care. I was separated from my family. My daughters were minors who didn't have an authoritative voice in my medical care. I felt vulnerable.

Dr. Rodriguez proceeded to show me a curved metal hook that looked like a large fishing hook and said to me, "We need to insert this IV into your neck. It is a more convenient spot to have it while in the ICU. You will have more freedom to move around. You probably are not used to this in Canada, but we do it all the time here."

I had never seen an IV stuck in someone's neck before. But I really didn't know any better. Looking towards the young lady beside me in the ICU, she had one in her neck. Assuming that it was more routine for them, and the medical students were witnesses and needing instruction, I said, "Ok, whatever you think is best."

I had a fear of needles to the point where, giving blood samples at my home clinic, I would need to lie down not to faint, and I actually fainted once before. I really needed to have this IV work the first time, so I cooperated as best I could. Dr. Rodriguez grabbed my neck around my jugular with his massive, meaty hands and squeezed tightly. He then guided the fish hook IV into my neck. I didn't feel much pain, just a sharp prick and then the slide of the IV through my tightened skin. Dr. Rodriguez then pulled the fish hook out and gave a little sigh.

"That one didn't work!" he said.

Not what I want to hear.

He tried again and again, still not finding the vein. The doctor, with frustration in his tone, told me to relax. I was as relaxed as I could be. I did not want this torture to continue; I just wanted it to be over, so I relaxed as much as possible. Dr. Rodriguez, grabbing my neck more forcefully, again told me to "just relax." I don't know how much more relaxed I can be as I am pretending to be asleep. Two more attempts, and he gave up. I guess the lesson didn't go as planned.

He said to me, "I apologize. I can't find the vein, and I'm not going to keep trying."

He walked away without saying anything to his students and proceeded to talk to the ICU nurses. Dr. Rodriguez, embarrassed in front of his students, left the room. The students looked at one another and shuffled out after him. Round two of the IV was then handed over to the ICU nursing staff. I didn't know if I was dehydrated or if my blood pressure was still low, but the ICU nurses had a terrible time trying to insert the IV. Four times on my right arm with no success, followed by three times on my left arm with still no success. I was a human pin cushion, my worst nightmare! Finally, they accomplished their task on the top of my right hand. After both my and the nursing staff's frustration with the IV, a woman came in to take a blood sample...*great*! After looking at my pin cushion arms, she decided it was a good idea to take blood from my wrist—I had never had a blood sample from the artery in my wrist before. *Another first for me!*

Friday Night, Reunited

They finally left me alone for a while. I was settled in my ICU bed, traumatized from what had just transpired, and hooked up to a machine monitoring my vitals and recording my heart rate. The IV in my hand was tender but tolerable. I relaxed, taking in my surroundings, and occasionally made eye contact with the patient beside me. The older woman across from me was still slightly curled up on her bed, eyes shut and unresponsive to what was transpiring around her. Two nurses came into the room and headed towards me. Standing beside my bed she greeted me with a big smile and said "Hello." I responded with a smile, not knowing why she was there.

She stood silently for a few seconds, then told me, "You stink, we going to wash you!"

Never had someone given me a sponge bath before, and it took two of them rolling me around and changing the sheets at the same time. The whole process was very well choreographed. Afterward, I felt and smelled much better. At this point, everything I had left the resort with that morning had been taken from me. My shoes, wedding ring, clothes, phone, watch, and glasses were gone, and I wondered if I was ever going to see them again. Without my glasses, the finer details of the room, like the writing on the walls and the details of the only television suspended from the ceiling, were impossible to see clearly. I was handed a hospital gown to wear. The hospital gown was not quite my size—my backside was open for all to see. Another gown the same size was brought to me to cover the back and drape off my shoulders like a dressing gown. There was no clock in the room, or anywhere I could see. I had no idea what time it was. The curtains on the windows had been drawn shut. I was bored and did not know what to do with myself. The old lady across from me stays still with her eyes closed. She does move from time to time with quiet moans, slightly repositioning herself. Her movement was all that reassured me that she had not passed away. I looked towards the young lady beside me and said *Hola* again. She smiled and waved. I asked her if she spoke English, and unfortunately, she did not. I thought to myself, *If I'm going to be here for any length of time, I'm sure going to be bored!* A nurse I had not seen in the initial introduction to the ICU walked into the room and headed straight toward my bed. She introduced herself as the nurse who was working upstairs in the tourist wing and was now the one who was looking after my two daughters.

"I am the nurse working upstairs with your daughters. Your daughters are very nice and very polite." She said with a smile. "They are being well looked after. They have a nice room to stay in, they are comfortable, and they are being given meals. Perhaps soon, they will come down for a short visit."

I desperately wanted to know how they were firsthand. I wanted to know how they were feeling and needed to reassure them that I was doing okay. I felt really bad that they were without me and probably didn't know what was happening, where I was, or how I was doing. Not knowing the time but understanding that a lot of time must have passed since they saw me last, I knew they would have been anxious and worried.

"Seeing them would be fantastic," I replied, relieved at the thought. "Let them know I'm doing ok and look forward to seeing them soon."

The ICU was very bright, with fluorescent lights illuminating already white walls, floor, and ceiling. A small table stood beside my bed, and there was a chair against the wall; a heart rate monitor and IV stand beside me, dripping the Amiodarone.

What the furnishings around me lacked in entertainment, the ICU staff made up for it. From my experience, the ICUs that I had known were all quiet and subdued. This Cuban hospital was the complete opposite. The ICU staff were incredibly noisy. If any patient needed rest for recovery, they were not getting it here! Voices were constantly echoing from the hallway, and staff bantering back and forth like they were celebrating and telling life stories at a high school reunion. Although entertaining, I had difficulty comprehending how beneficial it was to the patients who needed rest. A doctor with a three-quarter-length white coat entered the ICU and approached my bed. I guessed him to be in his mid-fifties. He was stout with thick skin and rounded facial features.

He introduced himself and then started to explain why I was in the ICU, "Your heart is weak, and you are on medication to relax and stabilize the heart. The medication you are on," he pointed to the IV, "is Amiodarone and it is used to treat Arrhythmia."

"I feel fine!" I said, in a tone of protest. I just wanted to claim my kids and get back to our valued vacation time at the resort. I continued, "I feel good enough to stand up and walk out myself. "

He said, "It is necessary for you to be on this medication for a while, and we need to monitor you while you are on this medication. You will most likely be here for three to four days."

I was devastated.

Immediately, I felt bad for my kids in their room upstairs. The only real vacation on our own, out of the country, was ruined. I was desperate for Louise to be here with Olivia and Lily. I could handle being cooped up in a hospital as it was my health issue, but thinking about my girls alone and afraid for their father was too much.

The doctor continued, "The ICU in Cuba is very different from ICUs in North America. Where you are from, ICUs are very quiet, and here in Cuba, we are very loud. Here, you will find we are very expressive, and we talk a lot. It is not quiet, and there is a lot of action going on." He finished by reassuring me, "The doctors are very good and know what they are doing, and you are in good hands."

Honestly, I was more worried about the nursing staff who were going to be looking after me in my day-to-day care. If the IV debacle was any indication of the type of care and professionalism I was going to have, I was not looking forward to the next few days.

The doctor who discussed my situation made no mention as to why I was left alone to wake up without care being administered. He didn't tell me anything about what they did to keep me alive. They were holding back information from me. The hospital was not being honest with me. I felt insecure in their care. I do not trust them.

I decided that I wanted to keep my death to myself. I knew that I had died, and I knew that they knew, too. I did not want to let on that I knew how serious my condition was. So far, nobody other than my dependent minor-aged children knows that I was alive. I had not seen them yet, so I was not sure what they knew of my condition.

Financially, I may have been worth more to them dead than alive. If my condition was not documented or known to anyone except my family, who knows how motivated they were to keep me alive.

I knew it was getting late in the evening, and I was quite hungry. All I ate today was a little fruit and some juice early in the morning before we left on our excursion. I didn't know any protocols regarding my stay or how or when to ask for anything. As my hunger pains start to ramp up, a nurse brings a tray with tin covers on it. I was a bit nervous about what they made for me and also excited that I was going to finally have some food. I knew Cuba was not a land of plenty, and many people were without basic necessities. I also knew food was sometimes scarce, limited, and occasionally rationed. I was not a picky eater, but I was also not that adventurous. The food presented to me looked surprisingly good. Everything was carefully portioned on the plate. There was the shredded protein that I guessed was chicken mixed with some onion and peppers, a small amount of rice, and some steamed sweet potato. The meal was also served with black tea and bottled water. The meal was freshly prepared, nicely seasoned, and tasty.

The young lady beside me proceeded to remove some plastic bags from a shelving unit beside her. The bags were filled with plastic Tupperware containers filled with food. There was no food preparation for the other ICU patients. Their food was prepared and brought in from the family. I felt guilty as I was the only one being provided hot, freshly prepared food. My right hand had the IV stuck into it, so I had to use my left hand and found it difficult to eat as I was right-handed. I took longer than usual to get through the dinner. Considering how little I had eaten that day, my appetite was not what I thought it would be. Knowing that having this food prepared for me was a luxury to the other patients, I got through the serving, and what I could not finish, I spread around the plate to show that I at least tried.

What seemed to be a couple of hours after dinner, a nurse from the upstairs foreigner wing came into the room to see me.

She walked to my bedside with a greeting smile and told me Olivia and Lily were doing well, and they should be able to see me soon. I couldn't help but create a big smile. I waited in anticipation for well over an hour before I saw the nurse again through the large window in the wall. As the nurse walked towards the ICU doorway, I saw Olivia following her into the room. Once in the room, our eyes met, and we both smiled wide. I was surprised not to see Lily.

Olivia got to the side of my bed quickly and stated, "Lily is fast asleep in the room. After such a hard, emotional day, I couldn't bear the thought of waking her."

After the day we had, I was happy to hear she was getting much-needed sleep. I had no idea what time it was, so I asked Olivia. She said, "around twelve o'clock midnight."

I was shocked at the time. It had been about ten hours since we arrived at the hospital. There were not ten hours of events I could account for. I wondered, *How long was I really dead?*

Olivia, knowing how important it was to spend time with me, sympathetically stated, "I want to spend time with you, but I don't want to stay too long in case Lily wakes up and finds me not there ."

I felt respect for Olivia's understanding and compassion for her sister. Olivia was growing up and becoming a responsible young lady. She was heading off to university soon, and witnessing her thoughtfulness and maturity towards her sister's emotional wellbeing, I started to feel slightly more comfortable with the idea of her leaving home. I needed her to be strong for both her and Lily. I sensed she was up to the task. Since Lily may wake to an empty room, our conversation got down to the facts.

Olivia had been in contact with Louise, and she was planning to come down to Cuba as soon as possible. Louise was not able to get a straight answer from the hospital regarding my diagnosis and condition. All she was told was that I had been in serious condition but that I was okay now and would be fine.

"Mom said she just about lost it on the phone," Olivia said. "The administrator who's been taking care of us told Mom they planned to have a driver take us back to the resort. Can you imagine?

"Mom told her, 'Under no circumstances are you going to release my daughters to some stranger to take them back to the resort. They are to stay in your care until their dad is ready to be released. They are to stay in that hospital and stay with their dad!'"

"That sounds like her," I laughed. "There was no way that she was going to allow the hospital to release you two minor girls to some stranger to drive you an hour away to the resort."

Olivia said to me, "Mom is hopefully going to get to us by Sunday morning if she is able to make all the necessary arrangements in time."

I felt such relief knowing soon, Louise would be here to claim the kids and take the burden of responsibility off Olivia. But I didn't know how Louise was managing this trip on such short notice.

I said, "Cuba is a communist country, and without any prior travel plans, I am not sure how easy it is going to be for her to get everything in order to arrive here." I continued, "Although, now that I'm hooked up to a medical monitoring device and IV, I am doing fine. I feel fine, back to normal. I feel good enough to leave right now, but they need to monitor me while I'm on this medication," as I pointed to the IV. "I don't know how long I'm going to be here. They said two, maybe three days."

I needed to offer more of an explanation of what had happened to me, but I didn't want to delve into the huge and emotional near-death experience. "After you and Lily left the room, I passed out. Everything went white, and I saw a bright light. When I woke up, I was back to normal, and everything seemed fine. When Mom gets here, she can probably take you and Lily back to the resort for at least a day or two on the beach."

Olivia smiled and, with a nod of her head, said, "We'll see."

The nurse came back into the room to say time's up. Olivia turned to me and said with a half-smile, "Well, I should be going soon anyway because of Lily. I'm glad you are doing okay. I love you! Both Lily and I will see you sometime tomorrow."

The nurse then escorted Olivia out of the ICU and disappeared down the hallway.

The lights of the ICU were turned off, and the room became slightly darkened to a dull grey hue. I slept well that first night, only waking a few times to change my resting position. The nursing staff were on 24-hour shifts starting around eight or nine in the morning.

During the night, the nursing staff slept at the desk in the room by placing chairs together and throwing a blanket over themselves.

Saturday Morning, Better Off Dead?

I woke up early the next morning. I wasn't sure how long I had slept as I didn't know what time I had fallen asleep or what time of the morning it was. It was difficult to get back to sleep, anticipating seeing both my girls again and perhaps some news from Louise. '*Is she going to make it by Sunday morning?*' I thought. I was feeling pretty good and stable, no different from the previous evening, and after I was sent back to my body by God.

The nurse sleeping at the desk curled up between two chairs was restless herself. She was obviously not comfortable, consistently moving to change her position. She was trying to stay asleep by covering her head with the blanket to block out the light coming from the brightened hallways. The nurses started moving around the hallways, making noise and talking with each other. The quiet talking slowly became louder and louder, waking the other patients in the room. Lights gradually came on throughout the ICU, and the nurses' voices rose to a crescendo, echoing through the hallways and making sure everyone was awake and alert.

A new day of hope was starting. I was optimistic that if I exhibited improvement and good, stable health, body and mind, the hospital would release me back to our vacation sooner than anticipated. Breakfast consisted of a hardboiled egg, dry toast, and warm goat's milk. I am not one for hardboiled eggs, but seeing the other patients in the room were not being provided anything, I accepted what was offered with gratitude. The nurses who delivered the food, standing beside my bed, watched me as I ate, and I tried really hard to conceal my disgust for the egg. I choked the egg down with the toast, and as I finished, the nurses smiled in satisfaction as they cleared my tray.

Later that morning, a nurse entered the room with a large syringe of clear liquid. It was huge, and I had no idea what was going to happen or where that syringe was going to go. The nurse nervously approaches the side of my bed. From my own nervousness and out of desperation, I think, *I'll rip off my IV's. Run out the door, turn left down the hall, and find the elevator. Get to my girls. Grab my stuff. Head out into the city to catch some kind of transportation back to the resort...building a raft out of found materials and sailing away towards Florida like thousands of Cubans had done before.*

I was on edge, contemplating my possible success rate of escape, when the nurse, not knowing English, said, "Potassium," and pointed to the IV inserted in the top of my right hand. Knowing it was going to go through the IV and not injected was a relief. The nurse inserts the syringe into the IV in my hand and slowly starts to push on the plunger. I should have built the raft! Suddenly, an overwhelming pain shot through my arm. Jumping and gasping because of the pain, my eyes glared at the nurse. There was no way it was to feel like this. She did not understand English, and I could not communicate effectively the amount of pain there was. She stared at me and slowly, seemingly bewildered, continued injecting into my arm. Again and again, it was like a tidal wave of suffering flowing through my arm up to my elbow. It was like my arm was being crushed under a steamroller. Again, my only reaction was to jump, and this time, I adamantly protested going any further with this painful foolishness. If she was to continue, I think I would pass out. I said, "No!" and defiantly shook my head and waved her off from continuing any further. I came to the conclusion that the IV had been compromised and must have gone through the vein. The

Potassium was being injected straight into my arm. The nurse, finally understanding the pain I was in, backed off, turned away from me, and slowly walked away, saying nothing. My right arm was immediately swelling up like a balloon. I watched my arm as the knuckles on my hand and my elbow almost completely disappeared.

Later that first morning in the ICU, the nursing and doctor shift changed. The new doctor was young and smaller in stature than the other doctors I had met. Introducing himself, he seemed nice and direct and had limited English but enough to understand the basics of a conversation. During our introduction, the doctor asked if I was at all dizzy, and I said, "No, not at all ." He then asked if I could walk around a bit. That was great news to me as I hadn't had to go to the bathroom yet, and I knew the time to go would be sooner than later. The new nursing staff were now predominantly in their roles, having taken over from the previous shift. The noise level from the staff escalated exponentially. I was anticipating a Caribana parade to come marching down the hallway. I guessed this new shift had been out partying all Friday night and still hadn't slept.

A large nurse who was the most sociable of the group and the center of everyone's attention sauntered towards me with a smile. "James Robinson," she shouts, saying my last name incorrectly. It was like an announcement so everyone could hear on the entire floor of the hospital. "Mr. James Aaron Robinson," she says with a widening smile. I sat up straight in my bed to appropriately greet her; I smiled and said one of the few greetings I know, "Hola, com es ta?" She breaks out into a deep baritone laugh. I think, *She must have heard about me being there or read my chart, which probably informed her that I didn't know any Spanish. My futile Anglo-Saxon attempt at the language amused her.*

She replies in a loud and commanding voice, "I speak a little English but not very well."

I assured her that her English was much better than my Spanish. I could see her thinking, straining in thought, perhaps trying to figure out a translation for something she needed to communicate. A few seconds passed, and I was anticipating something spectacular after so much thought before speaking.

She then intently looked at me, and with a smile and a slight laugh, she said, "James Bond, Hank Aaron, Swiss Family Robinson, that is your new name!"

As she repeated the name. Her laugh became louder and infectious to others and was heard throughout the room. The older patient across from me didn't stir. Satisfied with her creation of a new name for her patient, she turned away from me and walked towards the room's nursing desk. I assumed she was going to write down my new name on my medical chart.

I interrupted her walk with my own question, "What is your name?"

"Dwendy, Wendy with a D in front of it." She smiled and turned back toward the desk and her charts. Although not much rest was in my future, I knew that my Saturday in the ICU was going to be more entertaining with her personality around.

The nurse looking after my daughters came into the room and said, "Your daughters will be able to visit with you soon, after breakfast." I was delighted to hear I could see them soon, and my spirit was lifted in anticipation. I notice a male nurse on this Saturday shift, and he soon makes his way over to my bedside. He was around 5'10", similar in age to myself, with a thin build but fit, and had a nice, tanned complexion. He introduces himself as

Yoandis. Yoandis was soft-spoken with a very mellow tone, and he had good conversational English.

After we were introduced, he told me, "When you arrived, your condition was very serious and not very good. But you pulled through, so you must be here for a reason."

Later that morning, Olivia and Lily arrived, and I could see them through the large window displaying the hallway before they entered. Lily was following behind Olivia, and I could see the stress in her body language as she was apprehensively moving forward under the direction of one of the nurses. She was not relaxed and took the moment in by looking at her surroundings. She seems awkward, like walking through a carnival fun house, not knowing what was around the next corner or if something was going to jump out and startle her. Lily had never known me to be in a hospital. As Olivia and Lily rounded the corner into my room, I could see the relief Lily felt when she saw me alert and happy to see them. Lily approaches my bedside cautiously, looking at the other patients in the room, the monitors and IV I am attached to. The young lady beside me smiles at them and gives them a slight wave hello.

As they came to my bedside, I immediately assured them, "I'm doing good except for all this stuff," as I gestured to everything that was attached to me. "I feel fine. Back to normal! They are keeping me here to monitor my condition and make sure I'm stable."

Olivia then asked, "Do you know how long you are going to be in here?"

"I'm not sure, and they said at least a couple of days. I'm on this IV medication for my heart, and they want to make sure it is working."

I could see the disappointment on their faces. I would be disappointed as well. We were having such a fun time. There was so much more time to our vacation and a lot more to look forward to. This hospital stay was not going to be a quick in-and-out experience.

"I'm sorry for ruining our vacation!" They both are gracious and brush my comment off like what was happening was no big deal. I knew better and appreciated their support and understanding.

Olivia responded, "We are being well looked after. We are in a nice room with a nice bathroom and a balcony, and they are feeding us well."

Lily was quiet, possibly overwhelmed with what was happening and taking in all this information at once, realizing their vacation was going to be ruined, and their dad was okay but not okay at the same time. Not well enough to be released back to the resort but well enough that she shouldn't worry about losing me.

What I had experienced was burning me up inside. I desperately wanted to tell them how I had died, gone to a place with golden clouds, met my guardian angel, and conversed with God while in his radiant love, but the timing was not appropriate.

I remind them we don't have long together. The nurse made it very clear that visits to the ICU were not permitted. The hospital administration was making an exception as they were still minors at eleven and seventeen years old, and I was the only parent with them.

Olivia, responding more urgently, relaying to me her recent correspondence with Louise, "I have been in contact with Mom, and she is trying to get down here as soon as she can. She is hoping to get here by Sunday morning."

This was the best thing I have heard all day. It was such a relief knowing that she would be here for the kids, to support them and take much of the burden off of Olivia. I also longed to see her and needed her support to help get us out of Cuba when the time came.

Olivia continued, "The Canadian Embassy called and let me know they knew what was going on with you and that they were going to do everything they could to help us. It was hard to understand the Embassy lady, though, her English wasn't very good."

Red flags ran through my head regarding this call. I thought it was strange that anyone at the Canadian Embassy would not be fluent in English. Canadian Embassy staff are supposed to be Canadian citizens. Canada has two official languages, English and French. Olivia was almost fluent in French, so if it were a person from predominantly French-speaking Quebec, there would not have been a language barrier for Olivia. *Was it a fake call?* And why *did they call Olivia, a minor, and not Louise, my emergency contact?* I didn't even know how they got her phone number. It made me feel uneasy, but I tried not to let it show that I was concerned for my girl's sake. I didn't want them to feel like they did anything wrong or become frightened. I doubted anyone at the Embassy really knew of us and our situation. *Was the hospital trying to cover up something?*

Lying in the ICU, I was in no position to start making phone calls to try to figure it out. The hospital had taken all of my possessions, including my phone, and I had no idea where any of my belongings were being held. There was a part of me that hoped the call was real and that I would be taken out of the hospital and on my way home safely and supervised. There was another part of me that questioned the intentions of the hospital administration. I knew that hospitals received a lot more money for a dead body than a live one. An autopsy, cremation, storage, and return of remains would be billed to the Insurance for approximately eight or nine thousand dollars. This service is handled and administered by the Cuban hospital administration, and there are no third-party vendors allowed to take on this responsibility. Perhaps they were keeping my situation under wraps until they decided what was better for them.

Upon entering the hospital, my medical records showed that I had a zero percent chance of living. Perhaps they could try to keep my condition secret and then capitalize financially on that information. As long as nobody outside the hospital knew what my condition truly was, they had power and control over my life.

Before our time together was up, Olivia decided to call Louise from her cell phone so I would have the chance to speak to her directly.

Louise picked up right away, and the phone was handed to me. "Hi Hun, I'm doing okay, and the girls are visiting with me now."

"That's great. How are you feeling? What's happening?" I could hear in her voice that she was upset and was dealing with a lot of anxiety. "I feel fine; my heart rate is good, and my blood pressure is stable. I have an IV with some kind of medication for my heart."

"Are you able to leave the hospital soon? How long are you going to be in the hospital?"

"They said they are keeping me a few days, but I have no idea for how long, a couple, maybe three days. The girls are being looked after by the hospital; they have their own private room with a bathroom and are being fed."

Louise replied, "I talked to the hospital, and they are not telling me anything about your condition or what happened to you. Oh, he's fine but not fine. He's fine but in serious condition. He's okay but needs to stay in the ICU for a while. He was in serious condition, but now he is okay, we are keeping him in ICU… They were going to release the girls to some stranger to take them back to the resort!!! There is no way I'm allowing them to be released to some stranger. Could you imagine if they went missing?! I told them that there was no way in hell that they were separating the girls from you. People go missing all the time, and they are two young, attractive girls. There is no way I'm allowing them to leave the hospital without you!"

There was panic in her voice now, and I understood her frustration and agreed that it was not appropriate to release them to some stranger.

She continued, "Not knowing how long you are going to be in the ICU, not getting a straight answer as to what has medically happened to you, and not knowing what is to happen in the future for both you and our daughters is too much for me, so I decided to come down to you, get the girls, be with them and look after them while you are in the hospital. I can't sit here not knowing what is happening and wondering if I am going to lose any of you."

I absolutely agreed with her as I, too, didn't know what was going on outside the ICU and was not getting straight answers from the hospital staff.

She continued, "I'm taking Shiloh to your parents' place to look after her when I'm gone and try to get a flight out first thing Sunday morning. Hopefully, I will see you late Sunday morning. I can't sit here anymore worrying."

"I love you and look forward to seeing you, Hon."

"I love you too. I need to get going. I have a lot to do to get there in less than 24 hours."

Before she hung up, I had one last request, "Could you get hold of Pastor Lance and have him set up a prayer group for my health and our safe return home?"

"Absolutely, I will call him to let him know what is going on."

We hung up from each other, and I relayed the conversation to the girls. They both had a silly grin on their faces. When I asked why, they pointed to the monitor above my head and said, "When you were on the phone with Mom, your heart rate started to go up really fast."

We laughed together as the girls accompanying nurse said, "Perhaps they can see you again later this evening before bed."

Olivia grabbed hold of the railing on my bed in a show of defiance to leave that exact moment. She was not finished with everything she wanted to say. Lily stayed by Olivia's side, and the nurse backed away to give us a few more moments before escorting them back to their room.

"Dad, I have been in communication with my friend Shoray."

I knew Shoray from Olivia's school. They were friends in the same advanced program and had spent time socially outside of school on occasion. I had driven them a few times with friends to events and get-togethers. Olivia continued,

"Shoray's dad is a doctor at Brantford General Hospital. I told her everything that happened, and we were in a hospital. Her dad knows what is going on with us, and he said they will be ready and waiting for us when we get back. I told her we were returning Tuesday night, and she said her dad would be working emergency that night."

"That's great, Olivia. Thanks for reaching out and letting her know what's happening."

"I couldn't tell her much because I don't know what really happened. What her dad did say is that it sounds like something to do with your heart."

"Well, they first said faulty valve but are now giving me a medication called Amiodarone for something called arrhythmia. I don't really know either, and they haven't explained much to me."

"I said I'll stay in contact with her in case there is more information or any changes."

"Thanks, Olivia. At least they know and have a heads-up when we return."

The nurse returned and said it was time for the girls to go back upstairs. We said our goodbyes; the nurse escorted the girls out of the ICU, down the hallway, and back to their room, where they would either wait for my recovery and release or until Louise arrived to claim them.

Saturday Afternoon, the Bathroom?

Later that day, the male nurse Yoandis made his way over to my bedside and complimented me on my daughters. He, too had two daughters and showed me a picture of them on his phone. He opened up with me about his family, his wife, and his previous job making prosthetics for war veterans. He was soft-spoken and personable, and I could tell he enjoyed his work. He admitted that his work at this hospital was far better than making the prosthetics. He asked about my work and what life was like back home in Canada. He was quite surprised to hear that Canada did not have snow for twelve months of the year and that we actually had four distinct seasons and hot, humid summers. It was nice to have someone to talk to. A number of the women nurses, except Dwendy, stayed away from me as much as possible. Even Dwendy, when coming to check on me, did not have any type of conversation. Dwendy was pleasant, funny, and loud, commanding the conversation in the room, but did not ask any personal or thought-provoking questions like Yoandis.

It was Saturday, sometime in the afternoon, and the last time I used the bathroom was in the restaurant about 24 hours earlier. I curiously scouted around my bed, looking for any type of portable facilities. There was a stainless-steel bedpan shoved halfway under my bed and an old plastic liquid container placed beside the bedpan. I had never in my life used a bedpan, and I was definitely not about to without privacy. I already had everyone's eye on me as the foreigner in the corner. I could hold my backside for a while longer, not having ingested too much solid food, but the pressure from the waterworks was rapidly building and making me uncomfortable. I knew I could walk, and other than the IV holding me back, I knew I could manage a trip to the bathroom. I called for one of the nurses to come over. I knew the Spanish word for the bathroom was "Banos." I, as politely as I could, asked to go to the banos. My bladder was feeling quite full, and if there were going to be any prolonged language barrier negotiations, I had to start now. I knew the bathroom was not far down the hallway as the young lady beside me had been escorted there many times since I had arrived.

A nurse with very limited English asked, "Pee pee or poo poo?" I answered, "pee pee," and said, "banos" as I pointed to the doorway. Her answer was quick, without hesitation and without much thought, "No." She pointed to the plastic bottle from World War Two on the floor. The look on my face must have shown her that I had no experience with the technique of effectively peeing while lying down in bed.

She grabbed the plastic bottle and placed it under my blanket. This was going to be a new and challenging endeavor. I raised the back of my bed up to place myself in a more comfortable position and placed the plastic bottle, ready to receive a torrential outpouring. She left my bedside so I could continue on my own.

It was a steady, strong flow of released built-up pressure like rushing water from a hydroelectric dam. I watched the bottle fill halfway in no time, and there seemed to be no end to the constant and steady stream. The nurses were thoughtfully giving me my privacy, but I really needed to have the chance to ask for another bottle. Twenty-four hours without a pee break was too long. I couldn't stop myself, and I had to resort to creatively tilting the plastic container so it wouldn't overflow.

Luckily, by the grace of God, my bladder had finally emptied, and I had mere centimeters until an overflow disaster would have happened. I had a huge sigh of relief and was able to call the nurse over to let her know I was finished. I had to be very careful handing the full bottle over so as not to spill. The nurse looked shocked at the sight and a bit nervous. She grasped the bottle with two hands in order to keep it steady and not spill and had to concentrate while taking it from me.

Once she had it steady in her hands, she looked at me surprised and gave me an impressed nod for a job well done. When the nurse returned to replenish the bottle beside my bed, I noticed that this time, she had brought two bottles.

The botched potassium injection into my right arm resulted in an extremely swollen and sore arm. The IV in the top of my right hand was also very tender and sore. I informed the nursing staff of my discomfort. Yoandis came to my bedside to check it. He was concerned about the IV and informed me that they needed to move the IV to the other arm. As much as I did not want to be pricked by any more needles, my right hand was in pain every time I slightly moved it. My arm was also very uncomfortable staying in one position for too long. I knew Yoandis had compassion for my situation, but I still was not sure of his skill level at finding veins.

I prayed, "Dear Lord, please let him find a vein, guide him, and help him."

Yoandis checked over my left arm carefully. I must have been dehydrated as he had trouble finding a suitable vein. Eventually, he went for the easy one on the top of my left hand. The rest of my time consisted of a chest x-ray, ECG, and lunch.

That afternoon, the ICU was crowded with young students all in white coats following the attending doctor from bed to bed. About twelve students with a doctor approached my bed. I feel famous with all the attention on me and generally happy to have attentive visitors. The doctor was speaking to everyone in Spanish, but I could make out a little of what he was saying. My introduction to the students was very lengthy. Not fully understanding the language, I look towards the faces of the students to try and read their expressions, much like my first encounter with the ECG lady when I arrived.

Trying to follow the conversation and looking at the students, I received looks of concern, sympathetic grins, smiles, and surprise. They spent time discussing my condition, and there were questions asked and thoughts put forth by the students before they attempted to answer. It looked as though they were all quite perplexed, and they appeared to have a hard time with the questions the doctor was putting forth to them. I desperately wanted to be able to open up to them all and tell them what really happened to me and the true reason I was still alive. There was a difficult language barrier and a scientific barrier to break through in order to relay my story. I feared I would be placed on more different medications and admitted to a psychiatric ward. For my own good, God was keeping my mouth shut!

Shortly after dinner, the bedpan came back to my attention. I thought to myself, *there was no way I am about to give in and use that thing in this ICU.* I got a nurse's attention and asked to go to the banos. Dewendy was in the ICU and asked, "Ca ca or pee pee?" I said, "ca ca." She walked over towards my bed to check if the bedpan was there. Once she saw it, she pointed to it.

I looked right at her, shook my head, and said, "No! The doctor said it was ok, I can walk." While I made a two-fingered gesture of a person walking, Dewendy tensed her lips and raised her finger up in a gesture of wait while she turned to leave the room and consult the doctor. A few minutes later, Dewendy came back into the ICU pushing a wheelchair. I was so relieved that they were giving me the chance to leave my bed and go to the bathroom with some much-needed privacy.

I was wheeled out of the ICU, with toilet roll in hand, down a long unlit hallway. We made a right turn and went into another large hallway. There was an opening from that hallway into a bathroom. The bathroom did not have a door on it, and the wheelchair did not fit through the opening.

I helped myself up out of the wheelchair, and I went. The toilet was sectioned off with a half wall separating it from the main room with the sink. I turned to Dewendy and said thank you before venturing around the corner to the toilet. I turned the corner into the bathroom stall and suddenly realized that the bedpan would not have been that bad after all.

The toilet was well-used by many, unclean, and missing a toilet seat. There was nothing to support myself, and finding a clean place to set down my personal roll of toilet paper was out of the question. Someone needed to come into this place with a high-pressure fire hose and a hazmat suit. After giving so much fuss about not using the bedpan, I was not going to start to protest and ask if there was another facility to use. I wondered W*hy anyone would bring a patient to something like this*? *Don't they care about cleanliness?*

It was disgusting! I awkwardly squatted while hiking up my hospital gown with one hand and holding onto the toilet paper for dear life with the other. I finish as quickly as I can in record time. Heading back to the ICU, I was relieved that the bathroom ordeal was over, and I wondered how long I could last, holding my bowels so there would not be a next visit to that disaster.

Back in the ICU, the nurses had the blinds open, letting sunlight fill the room. Looking up the wall beside me and out into the natural light-filled courtyard between the cement walls and balconies of the hospital, I can see a beautiful, bright, blue sky through the palm trees. I longed to be out of the hospital and with my kids.

I imagined being with them outside, in the sun, and on the beach. They would be helping each other with their sunscreen in order to cover every part of their skin for the most, even suntan. In Canada, the tanning season is relatively short. The right tan can last longer, and inappropriate tan lines were to be avoided at all costs. We would have been wandering the resort, playing sports, going on nature walks, trying to get close and personal to the local wildlife. Olivia and Lily are nature and animal lovers. We would be swimming, tanning, and eating to our delight, relaxing and enjoying the sunshine while the snow and ice would be continuously forming back home.

Although the view outside the hospital window was nice and welcoming, it also made me sad thinking about my family not being together and enjoying the outdoor weather.

Being stuck in the ICU, the only thing that I could do for my family was to be as normal, friendly, and healthy as possible. I must be as cheerful as I could. I needed to show the hospital staff that I was back to my normal self, and then perhaps they would feel comfortable enough to release me and my kids so we could get back to the resort and try to salvage what was left of our vacation. This was my job and my new mission. Knowing my predicament where the outside world did not know anything about my condition except my kids, I needed to win favor with the hospital staff.

That afternoon, a number of people showed up outside the window. They were the families of the ICU patients. I guess it was visiting hours, but only from outside the building. There must be a walkway outside, under the windows. The window was crowded from wall to wall. Young and old, children and grandparents showed up to look in and support the patients in the room. There was no verbal communication as the windows did not open. The families could only smile, act excited, make hand gestures, and wave. The elderly lady across from me acknowledged her supportive family by the slightest of waves.

The young lady beside me quite enjoyed her family being there to support her. I am in the middle between the young lady and the window with her family looking in upon her. I tried to mind my own business and let them have their moment together. She was a mother and had a child less than a year old. Her family was looking after her daughter while she was in the ICU. I did not know what she was dealing with, and I did not ask. I knew that she was having difficulty with her lungs, as she would periodically cough up mucus and spit it in a bucket beside her bed. The doctors would take chest X-rays, and many times throughout the day, they would press a stethoscope against her chest and listen. Her breathing seemed okay, but she had a lot of mucus when she coughed. She was also hooked up to IVs.

After the window visitors left, it was time for dinner. I was prepared for a very similar meal of shredded protein with peppers and onions, rice, sweet potato, black tea, water, and warm milk. The meals were well portioned, and trying to be polite, I struggled to finish everything.

Saturday Evening, Dishonesty

The once bright blue sky outside started to dim, and shadows against the walls of the hospital became elongated. It was beginning to become dusk, signaling the end of the day. *Another beautiful, sunny, hot day wasted inside the ICU. My daughters must have been so frustrated being cooped up in a hospital room while looking out on a perfectly warm summer-like day,* I thought.

Soon after I finished my dinner and the brightness of the sun disappeared, I could see my daughters walking down the hallway through the ICU window. Not being able to see them all day broke my heart, and I thought of them often, wondering what they were doing to entertain themselves stuck in a room. They told me they were doing well, but I could tell they were stressed. They looked tired, and I could sense a nervousness in their voices. I tried to be cheerful for their sake.

They said that they were bored.

Lily told me of the game of hopscotch they made using the tiles on the floor and hair elastics. One of the nurses had brought, from her home, some movies for them to watch with subtitles. I found out about the number of phone calls that had been made. Mom had been in communication with them as well as the travel representative.

Louise told Olivia that she was going to be arriving at the airport the next morning at around 10 am. The hospital was about an hour from the airport, so hopefully, we would see her around noon. I was so relieved to hear that she was, in fact, coming to Cuba to be with us and take care of the girls. Louise would be responsible for them and give them relief that they were not on their own anymore, and I would continue to be the best ICU patient possible so they would have favor with me and possibly discharge me sooner.

Once Louise got to the hospital, she would be another person to know my medical status. She would know that I was in good health, the worst was over, and I was making a great recovery. My medical records showed that I should have been dead, so I just needed another few hours to stay healthy and alive and not become another statistic with a large payout to the Cuban Government attached to it.

The upstairs nurse came into the ICU and said it was time for the girls to leave. We said our goodnights, and they were ushered out of the room and disappeared down the hallway.

That evening, Yoandis asked me if I would like to watch a movie. There was a mounted flat-screen TV high on the wall opposite me beside the nurse's desk. Although I didn't have my glasses with me, distance was easier for my eyesight. I was bored out of my skull from being in bed for the last day and a half, so I welcomed the idea. The movie was a current title, bootlegged and stored in his phone. Thankfully, the movie was in English with Spanish subtitles. About halfway through the movie, I felt emotionally and physically exhausted. My eyes kept closing for longer and longer periods until I had to submit to the calling of sleep. I called Yoandis over, thanked him for the movie, and apologized that I was just too tired and couldn't continue watching. Within a few minutes, I was fast asleep.

Sometime in the middle of the night, I woke up. The room wasn't completely dark, but a light grey was cast throughout the room. I was on my back with the bed slightly inclined. My first point of vision was toward the nurse's desk. One of the women nurses was lying stretched across the desk, kissing Yoandis while he was sitting in the chair. It wasn't a quick friendship type of kiss. It was a prolonged make-out session.

The woman was not part of my ICU nurse team, but I did recognize her from the turnover of nurse staff from the previous day. From the morning staff turnover meeting, this woman seemed more playful, mischievous, and flirtatious and seemed to give more attention to Yoandis than the shift supervisor. I thought to myself that these two got along well and must have enjoyed working together, making the most with each other out of the long twelve-hour shift.

Knowing Yoandis had a wife and kids that he said he loved and cherished, the midnight sight of these two being intimate shocked me. Yoandis and this lady heard me shift in bed and immediately stopped to look over towards me. They saw that I was awake and facing towards them. I immediately turned over in my bed. I wanted to give them the idea that I was merely turning over in my sleep and did not witness anything. I initially felt bad that I may have caused them to be uncomfortable and perhaps embarrassed.

As I lay there quietly, about to fall asleep, I couldn't help but think about the dishonesty surrounding me. Yoandis portrayed himself as a loving family man, and here he was, ripping that notion to threads. *Who was I to trust?* The doctors were not upfront with me and not telling me anything that had happened after I had left this earth. *Why did I wake up alone in a dark room? Why did they not try to resuscitate me? Why the fake embassy call to my daughter?* Something was not right, and now, a man who was put in charge of my care and that I felt comfortable with was also a hoax.

I felt I was in a dangerous place with dishonesty at every corner. I was exhausted from the stress, and after a few minutes of being turned away from Yoandis and staring at the white cinderblock wall, I fell back to sleep.

The next morning, Yoandis approached my bed to say good morning. He pointed towards me and laughed, saying, "You slept very well last night, very, very well."

I took this as a comment regarding my snoring, which Louise describes as a Freight Train shaking the walls and windows. I laughed and concurred, "Yes, my snoring is really loud."

To make Yoandis not feel uncomfortable with what I woke up to the previous night, I asked him to kindly hand my glasses to me as "I couldn't see much without them."

It was the morning of Louise's arrival if everything went well with her arranging last-minute travel plans. I was anxiously waiting for the hours to pass until she arrived. I guess they knew she was going to arrive as Yoandis came to me and stated that it was time for me to shower and get clean.

The IV was removed, and I was placed on oral medication instead. My arms were very sore, and taking out the IV was a welcome relief. Without the IV, the proposition of a shower seemed less daunting of a task. A wheelchair was brought into the room, and after gathering a towel and bar of soap from my bedside table, we headed out of the ICU and down the long-darkened hallway. We turned into a room that was set up as a staff room with a table, chairs, and lockers. Beyond the staff room was a section of two showers. Yoandis made sure I was able to get my robes off, and I was left to my own devices. The showers were white cinderblock walls and clean tile. There was also a toilet in the room, and it was clean. *Why wasn't I allowed to use this bathroom earlier rather than that disgusting shit-stained bio-hazard I was brought to fifty feet away from this beautiful, clean space?*

I didn't complain as I enjoyed feeling clean and relaxed without thinking about having to take a tetanus shot. Returning to the ICU, it was almost time for the 24-hour staff turnover. I noticed my personal belongings had been brought back to me and were placed beside my bed. Yoandis gave me his email and said he would like to keep in touch and that he considers us friends now. It was nice to hear that in such a short time, I had made a good impression on someone.

The new nursing staff lined up inside the entrance of the ICU near the nurse's desk and were being briefed for their twenty-four-hour shift. I noticed right away that this group of nursing staff is a lot colder in personality. The dynamics of this group were more subdued and military-like, whereas the previous shift with Dwendy and Yoandis was very carefree, loose, relaxed, and social. There was one small, statured lady in the group who caught my eye. She was a very hard-looking woman. What she lacks in height and stature, she makes up for with a look that someone would not want to cross. She was lean, strong, middle-aged, and had a resting face that you would have a hard time chiseling a smile out of. *ICU round three should be interesting.*

Once the morning meeting was over, the nurses dispersed to their assigned stations, and to my luck, the tough-looking, hard-faced, bitter woman took position behind the nurse's desk in our ICU. She started talking to some of her co-workers in a disgusted, upset tone. During her conversation with the other nurses, she kept looking over towards me with squinted eyes, nodding and saying "Americano" in a tone of disdain. I'm sure she was not referencing the espresso drink. Every time she mentioned "Americano" and gestured toward me, I made sure she knew I was listening, and I replied loudly, "Canadian"! Even after my rebuttal correcting her mistake of my Nationality, she still continued talking about me referencing "Americano."

I knew that Americans were not well-liked in Cuba. Many Cubans blame America for their hardship because of the embargo against them and their Communist government. She seemed angry that she had drawn the short straw and had to tend to the strange foreigner. This woman sneering at me, obviously upset with the idea of having to be in the same room with me and needing to tend to me, made me feel very uncomfortable. I wasn't sure how I was going to get through the day with someone showing such open hatred at the idea of me being there. How was I to sleep that night… one eye open?! If the hospital wanted to do away with me in search of more money and use me as mere additional health care funding, she would be the one to follow through, no questions asked.

I gave her the nickname "Castro's daughter." I was now even more relieved that Louise would be there soon as another witness to my health and my survival.

Looking over my shoulder towards the heart rate monitor, I noticed that there was a twenty-four-hour clock on the monitor recording the time. I no longer had my watch as they took it from me before I left this world and had not returned it. Seeing that it was 11 a.m., I knew that Louise would be there soon and hopefully come to visit along with Olivia and Lily.

This sunny Sunday morning breakfast was served and consisted again of a hard-boiled egg and some dry toast with tea and warm goat's milk. Castro's daughter was the one supervising my breakfast and stood beside my bed, watching me intently as I took bite after bite of the egg and toast like a chef awaiting approval from a food critic. Hard-boiled eggs usually make me gag, but there was no way I was going to show any signs of dislike towards what they had brought me. Castro's daughter, after many attempts to smile as I choked down the egg and toast, seemed satisfied at my progress, uncrossed her arms, and left me to finish without saying a word to me.

After breakfast, I tried to communicate with the young lady beside me. With what little, broken Spanish I knew from listening to conversations and TV time with my kids when they were younger watching Dora the Explorer, I was able to ask her a couple of questions about herself. She had a baby boy about a year old, and her family was looking after him while she was there. She was suffering from some type of lung infection. She would cough up phlegm with a raspy sound coming from her throat. I did see an x-ray they took of her chest as they held it up to the light above and could see that her lungs were cloudy. Other than the coughing, she didn't seem to have much trouble breathing, and for the most part, she seemed in good spirits. During that Sunday morning, the curtains had been drawn to the side, and behold, above my bed, there was a paparazzi of the family all scrambling to take a peek at her, wave, and shout words of encouragement and love towards her.

The older lady across from us also had visitors, but she was pretty weak and did not interact much with her family. The odd time she would glance up towards the window and lift her frail arm to acknowledge their presence, it looked as though there were three generations that came to support the young lady. I wondered how they got outside the building and up to such high windows. They must have had benches on a balcony. The people didn't seem too steady, and several times, people suddenly disappeared like they had fallen down from the window. After their outside visit, I commented to her that she had a beautiful family. She smiled and said, "gracious."

Seeing her family there to support her made me want Louise to arrive soon. I felt lonely not being able to see my family my kids. Only having visited twice a day was hard. I told the nursing staff that I was very thankful for the exception of letting my daughters come into the ICU for a visit and let them know my desire to leave the ICU as early as possible so I could be with them.

Later that morning, a few nurses came into the room with a doctor and started prepping the older lady across from me for surgery. As they wheeled her out of the room, I knew from her apparent old age and physical strength, or lack thereof, that she had a slim chance of making it through and perhaps not seeing her again.

I said a prayer for her as she left the room, "God, please look after her and help the doctors perform to the best of their ability. If it is not her time, then let her pull through whatever she has to go through…amen."

The young lady beside me was watching them wheel the old lady out of the room, and as she passed by, the young lady looked over towards me with a concerned look. She didn't trust the potential outcome to be in the old lady's favor. She looked worried for the old lady and gave me an "Oh well, there she goes for good" kind of look. It was like she knew that once someone left for surgery, they rarely came back.

Sunday Afternoon, Louise Arrived

I finally saw Louise through the ICU window, walking towards the door.

A number of emotions ran through me before she even got inside: Excitement to finally see her, relief that she was there, and now our children would not feel the same burden as they have on their own, a bit of remorse that I had put my family through this; and, I knew that although Louise was here In Cuba and with her family, it was the last place she wanted to be.

Louise had arrived a bit earlier and left the girls upstairs in their room so she could be alone and candid with me about what had happened, how I was feeling, and if there was a diagnosis or prognosis.

She knew that I would have held back any information that would have upset them, not to make them worry more than they already were, and not to stress them out. As parents, we were there to protect and nurture our children and not cause undue harm or stress to them. Louise wanted the truth about how I was feeling and wanted to know what to expect in the coming couple of days left of our trip. Louise was not there on vacation. She was there to be with Olivia, and Lily took charge of what needed to be done to get us all home safely.

To help her, she needed information that she was not getting back home. Unfortunately, I was not given much information about anything. I truly did not understand fully why I was still in the ICU. I had felt back to normal ever since I returned to my earthy body. I felt okay, my arms were sore from the misplaced

IVs and the potassium injection into my right arm, which was still incredibly swollen. We were worried about how much time I needed to be there and how long they were going to keep me as it was already Sunday, and our flight back home was Tuesday evening.

I didn't tell Louise about my death and my experience in God's presence. Louise was already dealing with so much, and I did not want to upset her or stress her out any more than she already was. All that I could relate to her at that moment was that I was feeling fine, back to normal, and I didn't know how long they were expecting to keep me. I decided to wait and not tell her about the near-death experience until we were together and in a more comfortable environment where I could express freely and discuss, separate from the hospital's medical team.

The hospital was well aware of our flight time home because each doctor who had visited me in the ICU had asked. Louise said that there was no way they were going to leave without me, so everything had better work out over the next couple of days. She said that she was going to take the girls back to the resort for a little while to get them out of the hospital room, get some clean clothes and personal stuff, and perhaps try to get some relaxation after everything they had been through. I thought it was a fantastic idea.

As Louise and I were talking about the next couple of days, the elderly lady across from me returned from the operating room. She was quiet, sleeping, and not yet awake from the anesthetic. They wheeled her bed back into position across from me. They had monitors around her bed and a ventilator. There were three nursing staff changing her position in the bed to make her more comfortable. The old lady's sun-darkened, leathery skin was in deep contrast to the new white sheets tucked around her. She looked small in the bed. Silent. Two of the nurses left, and one nurse stayed behind to check and make sure everything was hooked up properly to ease her transition back from surgery.

I decided that while I had Louise here, she could help me make it to the bathroom, and I wouldn't need to rely on the nursing staff. I was sure this new group of nurses would make me use the chamber pot. Louise went to get a wheelchair for my trip down the hallway.

I watched the nurse tending to the old lady's attempt to hook up the ventilator. She had hold of two oxygen tubes, one in each hand. She was trying to fit them together and struggling to make the connection between the two tubes. The nurse tried a few times to get the two tubes to fit together, and I could tell she was becoming frustrated. I heard the oxygen escaping as the two tubes kept coming apart. Louise came back into the ICU with the wheelchair, and as we were about to leave, the nurse with the ventilator took one last long look at the two tubes, then frustrated, threw them in the air, shrugged her shoulders, and walked out of the room.

Louise wheeled me out of the room right behind the nurse. It was a quick trip to the bathroom, and when we arrived back, a privacy screen had been placed across the old lady's bed area. We no longer heard any beeping coming from the monitor equipment or oxygen from the ventilator. It was eerily quiet. I looked over to the young lady beside me, and she somberly shook her head.

The old lady had passed away. I felt dread, like I had witnessed a murder. I had assumed the nurse would have gotten help and they would have fixed the ventilator. The way the nurse left the room without any sense of urgency suddenly made sense to me.

They didn't care! They let her die! The Cuban nurse gave up and left this lady just like the doctors and nurses had given up on me and left me without trying to revive her. *What was with this hospital? This country? Do they not value life? Is life just another mouth to feed, a burden on the communist government?*

I felt for the woman's family, who had visited her at the window the day before. They were waving support for her, and now they would never see her again and would not know that the hospital did not do everything they could to help her survive. Knowing exactly where the old lady was at that moment, I felt relief at her passing. I trusted she was experiencing the love I felt, the peace and absence of pain. She was in God's radiant love, His embrace surrounding her. Her soul was completely free from the frail, weathered body that had many hard-working years accumulated on it. Knowing where her soul was, I said a prayer for her. Maybe God would let her hear my prayer like how he let me see my daughters. I said a prayer for her family as well so that they may feel comfortable with her passing.

As some nurses came into the room to remove the body, they mentioned to Louise and I that it was time for us to part ways. We said our goodbyes, and Louise said she would see me later that night. They were not going to stay at the resort but be back at the hospital to stay close to me. I appreciated the thought of them being close by and said to go have fun. The rest of that Sunday was me lying in bed reading, eating, and getting the odd check-in from the nurses.

The new doctor on duty I immediately recognized as one of the doctors who entered the examination room upon my arrival and was there beside my bed when I died. He was an older, grey-haired man with a military-style brush cut and around 60 years of age with dark-rimmed glasses. He came to me and asked, "How is everything"?

"Everything is fine. I feel fine, and I'm doing well," I replied.

He asked, "Do you remember me?"

I said, "Yes, you were one of the doctors I had in the examination room when I first arrived at the hospital."

He seemed pleased. While slightly nodding his head, he said, "You are doing very well. You were not doing well when you arrived, very serious, but now you are doing well."

I said, "Thank you. I feel like I'm doing well."

Hopefully, this doctor was on my side with his assessment, and knowing how well I was doing, he would release me out of the ICU and to my family. The doctor, unfortunately, was not a man of many English words, and I couldn't have a meaningful conversation or plea with him. He finished our visit with a simple "Good" and turned away from me to resume his work with the other patients.

I knew it was becoming late as the sunlight outside was beginning to fade. They brought my dinner of shredded beef with sautéed carrots, peppers, and onions with sweet potato, rice, and some black tea. I knew that Louise and the girls would be coming to see me that evening, and I was excited to hear about their day away from the hospital and Louise's first day in the tropics.

About an hour after dinner, all three of them arrived for a visit. I can see that they enjoyed getting out of the confines of their hospital room as they had smiles on their faces. The previous serious concern had subsided, and their demeanor was more relaxed. Seeing the three of them together for the first time since being in the ICU and observing some happiness with their mom was what I really needed to see. My spirits are lifted knowing they are at least out of the hospital and are more comfortable, knowing I am continuing to be stable. Their day back to the resort was not as much of fun as I had hoped. We were expecting to be back at the resort the night of the excursion, and we did not have any essentials with us. While Louise took care of important phone calls back home and got caught up with emails, the girls gathered some important items from our luggage, had stress-releasing baths, and brushed their teeth. They only took a few precious minutes to walk around in the fresh air and take a walk down to the beach. Taking a view of the Caribbean Sea and digging their toes in the soft, warm sand was important as they did not know when and if they were going to have another opportunity to do so for the rest of the trip.

As we continue to chat about their day, a nurse comes over, and we are told, "I have been told by the doctors that you will be moving out of the ICU sometime tomorrow. You will continue to recover in the same room as your family upstairs in the tourist wing. Your IV has been removed, and you will be taking oral medication from now on. We will still be doing regular checks the same as we do here, but at least you will all be together."

Last night in ICU! I should sleep well knowing that when I wake up, it will be a new day of excitement, spending time with my family, all of us together. I was tired and bored from a day of bed rest. It's amazing how someone can get tired from doing practically nothing. It must have been the stress I was going through that made me tired. Prompted by the nurse, time was up for our family visit. Louise and the girls left the ICU to go back upstairs and hopefully get a much-deserved night's rest.

I still had not told anyone of my time with God. I knew I had died on the examination table, but I didn't want to cause any undue stress on my family. I didn't want them to know how bad and severe my condition was until I was for sure stable, out of the woods, better, and recovered. I didn't know how I was going to deliver the news of my experience or even when. I did know that I would at least need to be out of the isolation dangers of the ICU and comfortably back with my family. I needed to prove to everyone that I was okay enough to be taken out of the ICU before I announced my death to any family member. I knew that the doctors and nurses in the hospital had knowledge that I had died, and they were not telling anyone either. The fact that they did not tell anyone the details of my serious condition was a warning sign that made their intentions with me and my care unclear.

Until I was released from the ICU, I did not feel fully safe at their government's discretion. My experience so far was that everything was about money and that they did not truly care about human life. The old lady's death across from me was a perfect example of not caring. It was a simple tube that needed to be attached to provide adequate oxygen. If the tube does not fit well together, you act with urgency to fix it and save a life! Nobody apart from my immediate family knew that I was okay and doing well. My insurance company had not been informed of my condition, or else they would have airlifted me out of Cuba and back to Canada for treatment. At least that would have been more of an exciting trip for my daughters to fly in a small plane back home rather than sitting in a hospital room for days. I had one more night in the ICU.

The nurse who had sneered at me and called me "Americano" was in the ICU for the night, and I wanted to sleep with one eye open because of my mistrust and continued position of vulnerability. It wouldn't have taken much for something to have happened, and they relayed the news to my family that I unfortunately did not make it through the night.

I could easily imagine the conversation, "I'm sorry, but your husband had a bad night, and his heart again went into arrhythmia. We did everything we could, but his heart was too damaged. We tried everything, and we could not revive him. We have taken him to the morgue for an autopsy. The autopsy and transportation of the body back to Canada will be nine thousand dollars plus another seven thousand for the care we gave to him and your daughters. You must pay before you leave the hospital, or we will be forced to hold you here."

I was—to say the least—a bit on edge that night. Not having complete faith in my caregivers' abilities and the non-transparent administrative powers of the Communist Government, who I was in the care of, would have much more significance had I not just had my near-death experience and interaction with God. I rationalized that why would God let anything happen to me so soon after saving my earthly life. Why send me back for such a short amount of time if something nefarious was going to happen to me? I had to trust in God that I would be okay and that I was meant for something bigger and more profound than lying in an ICU for a couple of days.

I woke up quite a few times throughout the night, not knowing what time it was. The heavy curtains were still drawn across the outside windows, and the lights turned off. Every time I woke, I would look over towards the nurse's desk and, again, see the night nurse struggle to stay asleep in the straight-backed old wooden chair blankets over her head. I had a restless night in anticipation of leaving the ICU and being with my family. Perhaps I could have one last day at the resort with them, laugh, have a walk on the beach, eat some different food, go for a swim, and enjoy some February sunshine on my face.

Gradually, upon waking to uncomfortably turn myself onto my opposite side, more and more movement and talking came from the hallway. Towards morning, there would be a lot more noise, nurses bustling around doing their morning checks, chairs scrapping across floors, talking, and closet doors opening and closing. Eventually, the lights would come on, and there I was, sitting up straight, ready for the day with a smile on my face. I knew that today, Monday, was the day that I got to leave the ICU and join my family.

Monday Morning, Being Wheeled Out

Something has happened to the demeanor of the "Americano" nurse this morning. She seemed much more pleasant towards me and even gave me an odd smile. She does not know any English, so all I could go by was her facial and body language. I think she may have been pleased that I wasn't any trouble, physically or mentally demanding towards her or the other nursing staff throughout their shift. I think that I won her over or at least gave her a sense of relief. Perhaps she was happy that I was going to be moved out of her ICU. After breakfast, a group of ten students accompanied by a doctor approached my bed. The doctor called for my "Americano" nurse to come over and start the group discussion. From what I could gather, she updated the group on my condition and care for the last twenty-four hours. As she was talking, I could see her start to smile, and it looked like she enjoyed being the one in charge, the center of attention for these new young doctors in training. I figured that she liked the limelight with all the students around and recognition from the doctor. I made sure I smiled at her, giving her my appreciation for a job well done. Perhaps I wasn't such a difficult patient after all.

My own happy demeanor may have made a difference with her. I wasn't demanding or needy, kept to myself for most of the day, and always tried to smile and be appreciative. I was not a typical "Americano" patient, and I must have destroyed any preconceived notion of what a foreign patient could be.

After a few minutes of relaying my status, the doctor took over. There were a lot of questions being asked of the students and some debates as well. Looks of puzzlement and a few supportive smiles from a couple of the women towards the back of the group made me feel quite important. I wished that I could have shared my own experience and opinion with all of them, but the difference in language was too great a divide. Again, for my own sake, I didn't want the possibility of staying in the hospital psych ward if I told them what I really went through and who actually sent me back from the dead. Medically, I should have stayed dead. Nobody recovers naturally from the condition I was in. Same as the group the day before, the doctors, students, and nurses, based on the conversation about my case, were all having trouble. There were a lot of shrugging shoulders and moments of deep thought amongst the group.

I knew the answer to all their questions and inquiries but was not called upon for my opinion. I didn't know what type of reaction I would get if I did try to explain my near-death experience.

I knew that science played an important role in the Cuban Government and atheism was very prevalent in the population. Fidel Castro poured a lot of money and resources into medical research. My experience would have been met with suspicion, laughter, and perhaps a heavy dose of medication. Although I desperately wanted to tell everyone, I felt it would have hurt my situation and made it more difficult for us to leave peacefully and without another incident. The doctor and students eventually ran out of questions, and it did not appear they came to any solid conclusions about my condition.

The rest of the morning, I waited and read my book Louise brought from the resort and kept looking towards the nurse's desk to see if there was any indication of them coming over to release me. I was enjoying reading my book but getting more and more frustrated with every passing minute. There really isn't much to do as a patient in an ICU, and you become much more observant and aware of everything around you. I didn't want to interrupt the nurse's constant and seemingly endless conversations as I never knew if their talking was important or a casual discussion about their day. When I was a child, I was always taught not to interrupt someone's conversation.

The young lady beside me was not so patient, and sensing my frustration, she abruptly interrupted the nurses at the desk on my behalf. I heard the Spanish word for family in her sentence, and the nurses immediately came to my attention and assured me that I would be seeing my family soon. They said they would go and find out when I would be able to leave.

My ICU comrade knew exactly what my frustration was and stepped in on my behalf, interrupting a conversation that obviously wasn't important. This young lady, having a baby and a family of her own, became the "momma bear" of the room. I could tell she was getting frustrated with the lack of attention and respect we were getting.

I graciously looked over towards her, giving her a smile with a quick wink, and said, "Gracious." She smiled with a bit of a chuckle and replied, "You are welcome."

Another ten minutes passed, and a nurse showed up with a wheelchair. "You are going to be with your family now," she said. "You are moving upstairs."

I grabbed what little I had, a book, sandals, a watch, and a wedding ring, and gave one last appreciative goodbye to the young lady. I told her I would pray for her, making the gesture of my hands together in prayer. I then pointed the nurse to the door and said, "Vamonos." There was some laughter as I didn't know many words in Spanish, but the few I knew, I put to good use.

I felt incredible freedom when I was wheeled from the ICU and down the hallway. One last stop at the administrator's office to gather my ICU medical reports, then out into the hallways of the hospital and up to my family waiting in the third-floor tourist wing. The administrator in the small office was not happy. It seemed a bother for her to put my paperwork together and, upon finishing, looked towards me with spite. She was upset that I was leaving. Perhaps she feels she lost an opportunity to earn more money for her hospital and government health care system. There was no other reason I could think of that could make her angry for me leaving. 'Not my problem,' I thought to myself. I was heading to my family, and in about thirty-six hours, we were scheduled for our flight home.

It felt wonderful being out of the ICU. Being in the open-air hallways of the public area was refreshing. It was a sunny, warm day, much like most of the days in Cuba. The fresh air filling my lungs was uplifting. Feeling the warmth of the wind and hearing the orchestra of songbirds in the trees of the atrium lifted my soul. My time spent in the ICU was stifling with the constant buzzing and hum of the air conditioner. The ICU was a very cool temperature, something the nurses were not used to, so there seemed to be an ongoing battle between them and the doctors on duty. The nursing staff would turn off the noisy air conditioner, and then the resident doctor on duty would come in, make his rounds, get a frustrated look on his face, and proceed to turn it back on. The ritual was never-ending throughout my stay, and it was humorous to see the struggle for air conditioning dominance.

We finally reached the pearly, frosted glass gates of the tourist wing and pushed open the large double doors. Coming to an open door near the nurse's reception, the wheelchair and I came to a stop. Louise and the kids were all in the room and jumped up to greet me. I felt such relief to finally be with them and have a big smile to meet them. Hugs all around, and shortly after, the nurses close the door to give us much-needed privacy and quiet time as a family.

Olivia and Lily gave me a tour of their hospital accommodation with a bathroom and balcony. The room they were in was the room I saw when God showed them to me. It was before I needed to make my decision to come back. I had never been in this room before. The room I had been examined and died in was next door. Seeing this room made me chuckle inside as it was further proof that my time with God was real and that what I was shown was, in fact, real. Olivia and Lily were escorted here just before my passing. I recognized the blue chair where I saw Lily sitting, and it was against the same wall. The couch has now been pulled out to a double bed. There was a raised hospital bed for me and a small round table with two chairs. The bathroom has a clean, functioning toilet, including, to my surprise and delight, a toilet seat. There was a stand-up shower, sink, and mirror. Off the main room, there was a very nice, large balcony that faced north. For the next two hours, we were left alone.

We were able to get caught up on almost everything the girls and Louise did during the past three days: the time spent at the resort with Louise, the beach, and a taxi driver, which made the long drive exciting and somewhat dangerous. While at the resort, they met with our regular breakfast and lunch servers and advised them about what had happened. One of the restaurant servers made a point to come out to the hospital after work to pay a visit. She thoughtfully brought some juice for us. We returned her kindness with what we could. Not having much except our personal belongings, we did have a few packs of bubble gum for her children.

They filled me in with their stories like Olivia's first drink of a Margarita on the beach, hopscotch on the tile floor using hair elastics, and the crazy taxi driver that was assigned to Louise from the airport driving like a maniac, way too fast and probably should have been a rally race car driver. Knowing that I had a rough time in the ICU and perhaps envisioning the worst of their stay, Olivia and Lily both emphasized how good their care was. One nurse, sensing how bored they were, went home and gathered English movies and movies with subtitles and brought them to the hospital for them to watch. Olivia said that they felt really cared for. The nurses were kind, thoughtful, and compassionate.

As I was listening to their stories, I couldn't help feeling overwhelmed with guilt for taking my family on such a dramatic and forever life-changing trip. I excused myself from the room to be alone on the balcony. Having been inside concrete walls, confined to a bed, and with all the trauma I had been through, I needed to take in the fresh air and feel the warmth of the sun on my face.

From the balcony, I looked past the hospital parking lot. The parking lot was incredibly small, with very limited parking spaces. Instead, most of the parking area was taken up by a large bicycle depot that was very busy with workers coming and going, dropping off their bikes while attendants kept track of their precious modes of transportation. There were hundreds of bikes of all shapes, sizes, and colors. The bicycle parking was like a well-orchestrated symphony. The attendants have an incredibly organization system. People would drop their bikes off, and others would be picked up at the same time. Attendants would work like a valet and fetch bikes that were requested.

Beyond the small parking area, there was a large empty field of a few acres of green grass met by another road. Beyond the road was a group of low-rise buildings. The building is a school where I could see a number of children in groups and uniforms. They are middle-aged school children with white shirts and blue pants and skirts carrying backpacks and books. The windows of the school are open in hopes of letting some sort of subtle breeze through. I couldn't help thinking about my own children in their climate-controlled classrooms, filled with equipment for enhanced learning, playgrounds, groomed football fields, and colored running tracks with precisely painted white lines.

By contrast, this scene was simple, uncomplicated, and made up of only the essentials of learning. The road between the hospital and school was a sight of mixed decades of the last century. It was active with loud diesel busses going by, billowing black smoke out the back tailpipes, and turn-century horse and buggy clip-clopping by with their heavy hooves. The school was just finishing, and some kids with their parents brought kites to the large open field and proceeded to fly them high into the sunny sky. It was peaceful, and I started to feel more relaxed.

The ordeal I have just been through felt over. Finished. We can now resume our normal lives and put this crazy adventure behind us…or so I thought!

Olivia on hospital balcony

Monday Afternoon, The Truth

Louise told the girls that she needed time with me on the balcony. She opened the door leading out onto the balcony. We both stood looking out at the daily goings on of a small Cuban city.

"So, how are you feeling?" she asked. She had asked the same question before, but now we were alone.

I reply, "I'm feeling fine; I feel normal, like nothing has happened."

"That's good."

I didn't want her to feel like she traveled all the way to Cuba to hear that I was "fine." Louise continued to stand at the railing beside me, patiently and silently waiting while the sun warmed our faces to see what I had to say and reveal my thoughts.

"I didn't make it," I said in a very calm voice.

Louise, not reacting but patiently waiting for me to continue, kept looking out from our balcony.

"I didn't make it. I died in the examination room. I left my body and was somewhere else. I met God and was sent back."

Not startled or surprised at what I had just revealed to her, Louise said, "I figured there was something more."

The hospital was being secretive, not transparent, and holding back something that had happened that they could not scientifically or medically explain. What had transpired over the last few days was not simply a result of me having heart palpitations, going to the hospital, and then having them disappear.

Someone having palpitations and then ending up in the ICU for days did not make sense to her, and it wouldn't to anyone unless there was more to the story.

What was not revealed to anyone was that I entered the hospital with arrhythmia, a heart rate of around two hundred and twenty-five beats per minute that I had been sustaining for over an hour. My heart had stopped beating, and only my valves were pushing blood through my system by opening and closing. I was literally, 'The Walking Dead.' My body did what was medically expected, no surprises: I died. Case closed.

What was not expected was me coming back to life. The medical staff gave up on me, which they never should have done. The Cuban doctors, having been trained internationally, knew to exhaust all options of treatment before declaring someone deceased. They did not do that. They did not do anything except place a useless IV in my arm with saline solution in an attempt to rehydrate a dead person. They should have performed CPR until a defibrillator was found, and they could attempt to reset my heart rhythm.

Louise was not getting the whole story, and I felt, because of their lack of transparency, that they were trying to cover up their inadequate non-treatment. A perfect way to cover up what they did not do was for me to be dead like I should have been.

I told Louise everything that happened after my last bubbled words: "Jesus, Jesus." And everything that was communicated between God and me. I was given a choice, and as much as I was enjoying the peace and inviting love, I chose to be back with the kids. I apologized to Louise about not having her as a part of my decision. I felt that she, at that moment, would have been alright. Other than my children, everything and everyone else in my life, their significance in my life, fell away. It was just me, my consciousness, my personality, and my thoughts. Everything attached to this earth was gone. I had no identity outside of myself. My possessions, job, art career, nothing was with me to define me except what made up my soul.

Louise completely understood and said, "Thank you for coming back for them, and I'm thankful you are here with us as well. So, what now?"

"I don't know, I have no idea!" Louise asked if I had told anyone else, and I responded, "No, not in full detail. You are the first person I've told. I did tell Olivia that when they left the room, I passed out and saw a white light but no other details."

Louise and I embraced, expressing our appreciation for being all together again. Louise didn't want to exclude the children from us for too long and went back inside to let them know they were welcome to join us on the balcony as it was a beautiful day outside. There was a knock at the door, which LilyLily heard first and brought to our attention, "Mom, Dad, someone is knocking at the door!" A nurse had come into the room to announce lunchtime. I was quite excited at the idea of eating together without some nurse hovering over me. The only round table in the room was small, but we each found a spot to sit as the nurse wheeled in our lunch on a small trolley. The lunch and dinners at the hospital were consistently similar. Soup with vegetables, rice, sweet potato, and the ever-changing shredded protein with onions and peppers, beef, chicken, or pork. It was freshly prepared and felt safer than what was being served at the resort. A couple of times, we were treated with ice cream.

As we were all enjoying our lunch, there was a phone call for us from the nurse's station. Louise's race car driver, Chino, was waiting downstairs, ready to take Louise and the girls back to the resort for a second time. Louise asked for Chino to wait until we finished lunch.

I was not yet released from the hospital, so I was to stay back and rest while my family traveled back to the resort. They would have time to pack some luggage and perhaps spend a little time at the beach. This would allow Louise the time she needed in the resort room to make important phone calls back to Canada regarding our health insurance. Confirming my earlier suspicions, our health insurance provider was in the dark regarding my condition. They had no correspondence with the hospital and only knew of me being in the ICU through Louise.

I have the rest of the afternoon and early evening to myself in the new room, not confined to a bed. The room, compared to the ICU, was very quiet. It was nice having the solitude to read a book, rest, be on the balcony watching the outside world go about their daily lives, and be in prayer. I thanked God for this continued opportunity to be with my family.

It was late when everyone returned to the hospital. The sun had just dipped past the horizon, and the color of the sky was moving from dusk to dark. Louise and the girls happily entered the room. Talking quickly with some laughter mixed in, it was obvious their spirits and stress had been somewhat lifted. Louise brought half of our luggage with her as she would have had trouble bringing everything back on one trip the next day. Although it was late upon their return, the hospital had dinner ready for us.

There was another knock at the door shortly after we finished our meal. Yessel, the travel representative who had been the liaison for Louise when she was back in Canada, came into the room. I had heard about Yessel since I entered the hospital. He was the one in charge of communicating with the children, making sure they were looked after, and advising Louise of what little he knew regarding our situation. Yessel had a slight build and a tanned, darker complexion. Upon entering the room and seeing us all together, he seemed very nervous. Sweat was dripping off of his forehead. He had a cloth handkerchief in his hand, which he kept raising to his forehead and continued to dab along his temples. After saying our greetings, the conversations naturally progressed into casual, more social small talk. His sweating stops as we become more comfortable with each other.

I said, "Thank you for all your work with my family. I am very appreciative of your communication between the girls and Louise."

I could tell he had to think about what he was going to say before he said it. Yessel, a nice man and naturally a caring individual, not only had initial concern for my health and my family but also for our tour guide, Rosemary. Yessel was concerned about her job as some of the tourists had made complaints about the time spent waiting at the hospital for her to return to the group. Apparently, another group had gotten ahead of ours and set them back even more when they arrived at the boat ride event through the mangrove forest.

I was so disheartened to hear about the situation that Rosemary was in. From my understanding, jobs in Cuba are not easy to come by. To think she could lose her job over me, especially after all her concern and care for my health and my children. Without Rosemary with us, I definitely would not have gotten the attention and care that I so desperately needed.

Ever since my heart stopped the first time in the jeep, Rosemary continuously kept an eye on me and kept checking in on me, my condition, and how I was doing. She offered to take me to the hospital numerous times, and I would have been there a lot sooner had I not been so stubborn. When I finally said I should go to the hospital, she wasted no time getting the group together to leave, and we headed straight there with little time to waste.

If she had simply left me, Olivia, and LilyLily at the front doors of the hospital, we would have had no idea where to go to get help and attention. Rosemary took charge of my situation and made sure I received the attention I needed. She also took charge of my daughters and only left to go back to the group once they were noticed by the nursing staff, looked after, and taken out of the room. I was grateful for her care and compassion. She was my earthly angel that day!

Yessel asked if I could write a letter to the travel agency to help them understand the importance of her actions towards me and my kids. I told Yessel how much she meant to me and my kids, and I would absolutely write something on her behalf. I would write the letter and have Louise deliver it to the travel excursion office. Yessel was relieved and then bid us farewell.

When we were alone and settled in the room, Louise looked towards me, and our eyes met. I knew it was time to let Olivia and Lily know about what had really happened to me on that Friday afternoon.

Louise announced, "Girls, we need you to listen. Dad has something important to tell you."

They sat quietly and listened. When I was finished telling them what had happened to me after they left the room, I reassured them that God had a purpose for me and I wasn't going anywhere. They were both silent, amazed, and a bit unsure of how to react. They periodically glanced over toward Mom for reassurance that I was serious and not playing a practical joke with them. Louise gave them the nod of assurance that this was real and Dad wasn't joking.

Their reaction was not what I thought they would be. Hearing that I was really in dire circumstances must have affected them in a way that I did not fully understand at the time. I don't think they ever really entertained the idea that I was in a circumstance where I could die. As far as they knew, I was having a health issue, but it was okay, and they were keeping me under observation for safety reasons. They didn't know the severity of what I had gone through. The fact that I did succumb to my health condition made me mortal, and, in their eyes, I was no longer the strong, impenetrable parent of immortality. Life and death were circumstances that could change instantly.

Louise and I reassured them that I was better, we were safe, and we were going home to resume our everyday lives again. This had been an unfortunate circumstance, but God had our family's best interest and loved us unconditionally. God wanted our family to be together, and we needed to appreciate and trust that everything was going to work out for the best. The girls eventually smiled, and I could tell that they accepted the circumstance.

Olivia and Lily started to ask questions like, "Did you see God, and what did He look like?"

"I didn't see God, but I was with God. He was too bright. I felt God, and He was love, is love. His love radiated all around me and through me. It felt like I was in his embrace. He was a part of me, and I was a part of Him. We were together."

"What did He sound like?"

"I didn't hear God. God communicated by thought. God placed a thought in my head."

"What did your Angel look like?"

"My Angel was beautiful. It didn't look like a man or woman. It looked like a ball of energy with a force field and swirling bands of color going around it, blue, red, purple, and mercury."

After a number of more questions, they felt satisfied and comfortable with what I told them. It was getting late. It had been a long day. Lily looked exhausted, and the rest of us were quite tired. We settled for the night. I stayed in the metal framed hospital bed while the three girls shared the double pull-out couch. They all seemed pretty squished, but being so tired, they managed to eventually get to sleep.

The next day, Tuesday, was our day to leave Cuba.

Our flight was leaving at seven thirty in the evening. Louise and the girls planned to go back to the resort one last time. The girls could spend one last small amount of time at the beach next to the stunning turquoise-blue Caribbean Sea. While they would pack up the rest of our belongings from the room, Louise would also make necessary phone calls back home and check out of the resort. The plan was for them to return from the resort to the hospital in time for me to be released and then head straight to the airport. Our taxi driver, Chino, would meet us at the hospital to take the girls while I would be driven by ambulance.

Tuesday Morning, Bonjour

We had a restless night's sleep, partly from stress and over-exhaustion and partly from my loud snoring. Lily did not look well. Her eyelids were heavy, she looked pale, and she informed us she was feeling sick. We checked her temperature, and sure enough, she had a fever. Lily also complained of having an upset stomach, like she was going to be sick. Of course, Louise and I were sympathetic to her, but hearing that she was feeling ill was the last thing we needed. Louise's correspondence with the Insurance company revealed that the hospital had still not released my medical records, making it obvious that they were withholding them for the sake of me staying in their care and generating more income from my illness. We were afraid that if they found out that Lily was sick, they would keep her for observation and may want to admit her to the hospital, jeopardizing our return home. It was a terrible predicament.

Louise got very direct with Lily, "You cannot allow them to see that you are sick! If they find out, they may want to admit you and keep us here until you are better. We do not want to miss our flight."

Lily understood and tried her best to conceal her illness. Lily went to the bathroom to try to throw up and make her tummy feel better. When a nurse came into the room to check on us, Lily stayed in the bathroom to conceal herself. We made the decision to have Lily stay with me in the hospital room to rest while Louise and Olivia went to the resort.

Chino called Louise, announcing his arrival downstairs at the hospital entrance. We said our goodbyes, and Lily and I had the day together in the room that she had been confined to for so long. I felt bad for her. Although Lily slept most of the time Louise and Olivia were gone, I enjoyed being in the same room with her after being apart. It was comforting for me to casually look up from my book or the testimonial I was writing for Rosemary and see Lily resting peacefully beside me. Every moment with my kids was precious, and I appreciated their presence. When Lily was not resting, we had a chance to talk.

I asked, "Lily, do you have any questions about my experience and time with God?"

Lily rose from her bed and settled into the chair at the end of my bed. She thought for a moment, then asked, "What did it feel like to die?"

It was a good question as I never dwelled on the act of me dying, just what happened after I had died. "There was no pain. I was a little scared when I started to have difficulty breathing. I just laid back, rested my head on the pillow, and allowed the doctors to do what they could for me. Next thing I know, the nurses and doctors went out of focus, fuzzy, and the whole room lit up with bright white light, and then, all I could see was white around me.

I was a little afraid because I didn't know what was happening, but I was comfortable and not in pain. When God took me out of my body, it felt kind of weird, though. I felt like I was on a carnival ride like the tilt-a-whirl we went on at the amusement park, and you know when you get pulled back into your seat?"

"Yeah," she replied with a bit of a smile on her face.

"Well, it was like that. I felt like I was being pulled out of my body, and there was a little pop sound. It was kind of fun and didn't hurt at all!"

Lily had a smile on her face when I finished answering her question. I continued about the peace I felt in the golden clouds and that the whole experience was pretty cool.

I could tell Lily was not feeling well. She didn't have any more questions for me, and I knew she needed to rest, and I told her to nap. I assured her that I wasn't going anywhere and that I would be there reading or napping myself. Lily laid down on the opened sofa bed and fell fast asleep.

By early afternoon, Lily was still sound asleep. I perked up and went outside onto the balcony. I watched the kids leaving school for the day with their uniforms and backpacks on, the constant coming and going of people, and the hospital staff in the bicycle parking area either dropping their bikes off or entering the hospital all fresh with a bounce in their step or, leaving the hospital walking tiredly to gather their ride home. Horse-drawn wagons trotted by, followed by diesel buses and trucks spewing black smoke coming out of their tailpipes.

With all the activities of daily lives moving around us, I still felt at peace knowing that I was out of the ICU, enjoying the sunshine and fresh, warm air. I was with my family, where we supported and looked out for each other. I prayed and thanked God for my family and the opportunity to be with them. I thanked Him for giving me the choice to be with them and for Him thinking about the wellbeing of my kids. I also apologized for not wanting to continue with Him to His kingdom of Heaven. I struggled with my decision to come back as I thought that it may have been perceived as a rejection of God. I had to reason with myself that it was not a rejection. God gave me the choice, and He did help my decision by showing me Olivia and Lily back here on earth, alone and vulnerable.

I like to think that I made my choice on my own, but I cannot take that credit. When I was with God and in His radiant love, I was ready to stay and continue on towards Him. It would not have been the right decision. God showed me that family was very important to Him and that He wanted the best for my kids and family, too. While on that balcony, peaceful and in fellowship with God, I prayed that the miracle of my survival continued on towards my better health, healing my heart and the condition that caused my heart to stop in the first place. I also prayed for Lily and our safe return home.

As I headed back into the room from the balcony, a nurse opened the door. Lily stayed sleeping, and the nurse asked how many people to expect for lunch. I said, just the two of us, and seeing Lily was sleeping, the nurse backed out slowly through the door.

It was around one-thirty in the afternoon when the nurse came back with our lunch. I had to wake Lily up, hope, and pray she was feeling well enough to eat. I was not prepared or capable of eating two lunches if she did not want to eat. Lily slowly woke up. I noticed she looked well rested; her eyes were more open and wider, and the rosiness on her cheeks had subsided. Her fever must have come down. I asked her about her stomach, and she said that it felt better.

Before we had a chance to start eating, there was another knock at the door, and a man entered the room. At first, I thought it was a doctor, but it turned out he was a hospital administrator in charge of the finances. He informed me that they released my medical records to my insurance company, and they were waiting for confirmation of payment to the Cuban Central Health System.

He then told me that *I would be discharged once the payment showed up on their system*. Our flight was later that evening at seven-thirty. With a travel time of an hour to the airport and having to arrive a couple of hours early before the flight, it was already a bit of a tight timeline.

I had no idea how long the process took to have my medical records assessed and then receive authorization for payment. I texted Louise. She was the one who had been in contact with the insurance company. Louise called and spoke to the administrator who was in charge of our file. Louise told her how immediate and time-sensitive it was as our flight was in a few short hours, and the hospital was *not* going to release me or my daughters until there was payment confirmation.

The administrator looked through a pile of papers on her desk and found our file buried amongst other work. The administrator admitted that she did not know it was urgent and was glad we called, or else she didn't know when she would have dealt with our file. Twenty-five minutes had passed when the same hospital administrator entered through the door with a handful of papers.

They were my release forms!

I signed a release for the services provided to myself and my family. The papers totaled just over seven thousand dollars. I gave the paperwork back to the administrator. It didn't seem to be that much money, considering it would have been in the tens of thousands in most other countries. It was almost two in the afternoon, Louise and Olivia were not back from the resort, and the insurance company still needed to authorize and send payment to the Cuban Ministry of Health.

Lily, still not feeling well, was not able to eat much. I did not want them to question her appetite, so I said, "Finish as much as you can, and I will try to eat some of yours as well. We don't want them to know you are not feeling well."

Unfortunately, my appetite was not the greatest. We ate what we could and spread the rest around to make it look as though we had tried all the food.

As we were finishing, Louise and Olivia came into the room, carting the rest of our luggage from the resort. Louise asked, "How are you feeling?"

I said, "Fine," and Lily responded with an, "Okay, but still not great."

I told them, "We are still waiting for confirmation of payment before we can leave."

Louise assured us, "I have spoken to the insurance company, and they are working on it, and once it is approved, the payment is quick by electronic transfer. There is nothing we can do, and everything is in God's hands."

I went out onto the balcony one more time and prayed for the transfer of funds to be on time and for all of us to get home safely. We then started to pack our belongings.

There was a knock on our door, and a nurse entered with medication for me. I figured it was the last medication to cover the time before we got home, and I could get medical attention. It was to be my "medical chaperone." As I took the dose of Amiodarone, the hospital finance administrator walked into the room.

He had a smile on his face while saying, "The payment has been received, and you can be on your way. You will be taken by ambulance, Aaron, while the rest of your family and luggage will go by taxi."

I let out a sigh of relief as if I had been holding my breath for days.

A wheelchair was brought to the room. Although I felt fine, I knew it was for the patient to be wheeled off the premises. We thanked the nursing staff as we exited the white-walled tourist wing and then through the large glass doors into the open-air hallways of the hospital. As we continued through the hospital, I saw missing and stained ceiling tiles with neglected maintenance issues all around, including hanging electrical wires dangling from the ceilings. I was happy to be leaving.

Louise and Olivia took the safer route of the stairs down to the ground floor. Lily and I took the more temperamental, rickety elevators with doors that never seemed to be able to close properly. We made it down safely and met up with the others at the front doors of the hospital.

Being outside the walls of the hospital was a literal breath of fresh air, lifting my shoulders and my spirits. Chino was waiting for us and grabbed our luggage and placed them in the trunk of his car.

Louise and I had a discussion with the girls before heading into the waiting vehicles. Someone was to stay with me at all times. We didn't want to take the chance of Lily feeling sick while in the ambulance, so it was decided that Lily would stay with Louise and have Chino drive them to the airport while Olivia and I would ride together in the back of the ambulance.

The ambulance waiting for us was not your standard, patient-focused vehicle we see on the streets of North America. This ambulance was a gutted-out utility van with an old leather-lined stretcher placed in the back that looked like it had seen the days of World War Two. There was an old oxygen tank, a bench seat down one side, and a workplace first aid kit strapped to the wall, and that was about it.

Olivia and I entered the back of the dented and slightly rusted van along with another passenger. A woman who was quite upset and was yelling profanities in an Eastern European language that I roughly identified as Russian. The orderlies were trying to assist her into the back of the ambulance, as she proceeded to yell at them and slap their helping hands away.

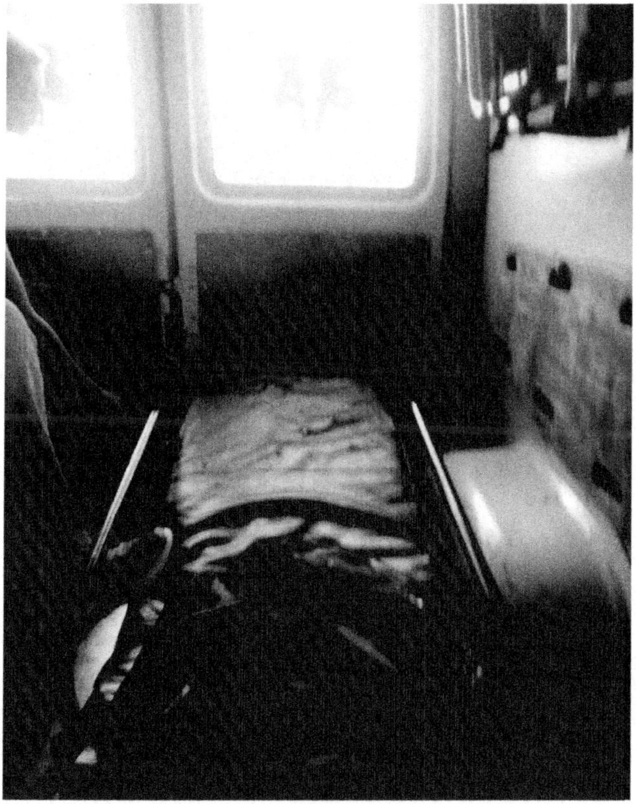

Cuban ambulance. Leaving the hospital.

In the ambulance. Right arm still swollen.

Olivia and I sat down where we could find a comfortable spot and looked for something, anything, to hang on too so we would not bash around the inside of the ambulance like the balls of a pinball machine. The paramedic, I think, or just someone along for the ride in the front passenger side seat, looked back at us through a small window and said, "Okay?" with his thumb raised. We answered "Si," and away we went.

The ride to the airport was wild. From the back of the ambulance, we cannot see what is coming in front of us. The roads must have been filled with obstacles, holes, animals, or small children playing as we swerved and darted like going through a minefield. We were being tossed around in the back with very little to hang onto while the ambulance kept picking up speed. The Russian lady got more upset and started yelling while being lifted off the bench from the bumps, and she grasped at anything she could hang onto. This was like driving through a war zone, not just a simple transfer to the airport.

I started to worry we would end up in an accident and be carted back to the hospital with injuries.

I was able to move myself towards a small window in the side of the ambulance and find something to stabilize myself. The ride eventually smoothed out as we moved onto the road across the estuary headed towards the resort district of Cayo Coco.

Although I was happy to be out of the hospital and on our way home, looking out the window at the different ecology of another country so far removed from what we were used to make me feel sad that we missed a large amount of time experiencing the diverse and different surroundings.

As we approached the airport, I could see the flow of tourists looking as though they had a great time, eating and relaxing in the sun, soaking up vitamin D, and here we were, climbing out of an ambulance with Dad being placed in a wheelchair. Accepting what had happened to our family was a hard pill to swallow.

As we departed from the ambulance, I was asked to stay in a wheelchair for the duration of our time at the airport. We were allowed to check in early with priority seating, at least that was one bonus! Louise's name was not on the original flight list, having been added to the flight after she arrived in Cuba. Most of the passengers were pre-booked with all-inclusive packages, and I guess it was very rare for a passenger to show up not coming from a resort. A couple of supervisors and about thirty minutes later, we were allowed to proceed through the customs gate.

Once through the gate and in the main terminal, we were told that the flight was delayed by a couple of hours. An airport concierge was assigned to me to make sure I was securely placed on my flight. He took us to the waiting area, placed us at our own private table near the elevator, and said he would be back to get us for our flight. After much-needed food and drink, the concierge showed up and told us to gather our things to board the flight first.

We emerged from the elevator on the ground floor and dodged our way through a crowd of people waiting to get to their flights. We passed through a barrier, with me in the wheelchair leading the way and my family following. Every eye was on us as we jumped the cue. We then went through a large sliding glass door that led us out onto the tarmac. There were three identical planes stationed in a row waiting to take on passengers.

The time was approaching past eight, and the sun had settled behind the horizon. It was quite windy, and I wasn't sure if the sound was the idling jet engines or the actual wind. The engine noise was high-pitched, and it was hard to hear anything my concierge was saying when we arrived at the steps of the plane.

This was as far as I was going in the wheelchair, and I was able to finally stand on my own to climb the stairs to enter the plane. At the top of the boarding stairs, three flight attendants greeted us. "Bonjour," they said through big smiles, and we returned the salutation with "Hello." They had a quick look at our tickets and showed us to our seats. We got our seats, which, amazingly, were all beside each other. There were three seats on each side of the plane, no middle aisle. I thought it fantastic that although Louise's flight was booked at the last minute, we were able to all be beside each other. Once our carry-on luggage was safely stored, we sat down excited in anticipation of leaving for home.

We were the first and only people on the plane.

One of the flight attendants approached us from the front of the plane and introduced herself as the head steward of the flight. I thought that it was nice for her to introduce herself to make us feel welcome. I had never had such personal service before. She then asked where we were headed. I thought it was a strange question as they checked our tickets as we entered the plane.

We said, "Toronto," in unison.

The head steward said, "Okay, this plane is heading to Montreal. You are on the wrong plane!"

Tuesday Approaching Midnight, Headed North

Montreal was a solid five and a half hours, five hundred and forty kilometers away from Toronto. "When we greeted you in French, and you replied in English, I thought I should check," she said. The steward rushed out of the plane to signal for another concierge to come back to the plane with a wheelchair.

Not knowing the status of the other two waiting planes, we hurried to gather our things and proceeded back out the doorway of the plane.

At the front of the plane, we were met by one of the pilots who came out of the flight cabin to assist us. The flight Captain introduced himself and apologized for the mix-up. He was middle-aged, tall, tanned, blue-eyed with blonde hair, and had an Australian accent. He was the perfect specimen for the old Pan-Am promotional poster. He assured us he would personally find the right plane. We thanked him and disembarked the plane.

The concierge proceeded to take us back to the airport terminal. We went back through the large sliding glass doors and, back in front of hundreds of anxiously waiting passengers who again had all eyes on us because of our special treatment. About five minutes later, the Pilot came back into the terminal and signaled for us to follow him. I couldn't help thinking that all the people waiting must have thought we were some kind of royalty with priority boarding and a personal escort to our plane by a flight captain. We arrived at our plane, which was at the opposite end of the line of planes. The captain assured us that he personally checked and that it was certainly the right flight. We thanked him, and off he went with my three girls, watching as he disappeared past the nose of the plane.

Again, we climbed the stairs to enter the plane and were greeted on the landing by three flight attendants. "Hello," they said through big smiles. We returned the salutation with "Hello," and we entered an empty plane.

We are finally able to relax and think about the pleasures of being home. By the time we were taking off from Cayo Coco, we had been delayed about two and a half hours, which had us landing in Toronto at around 1 a.m. Wednesday morning. We had seats beside each other and ordered hot food, which we had never done on a plane before, but we were very hungry. The rest of the flight was smooth sailing, and I was able to relax, not sleep but rest.

Disembarking from the plane, a wheelchair was waiting for me. I felt I could walk, and after being confined to a bed for days, I really wanted to use my legs. With the wheelchair being provided, I felt obligated to use it. There was no concierge accompanying the wheelchair, so Louise and the girls took turns pushing me around to our arrival destinations. Our plane must have been the only one scheduled for arrival early that morning, as the passengers on our flight seemed to be the only ones in the airport. By the time we had gotten through customs and gathered our luggage from the claim area, almost everyone from our flight had dispersed.

Traveling the large, long hallways of the airport was an apocalyptic feeling like most of the world's population had disappeared. Toronto airport was always busy. As we walked alone, our voices echoed as we spoke.

Getting closer to where Louise had parked our car three days earlier, Louise wheeled me off to the side while she went to ask for directions to our parked car and the quickest way out of the airport to get to the highway.

With her back turned and walking away, Louise didn't realize that she had stopped my wheelchair at the top of a slight ramp going downwards into a long hallway. I started rolling, said nothing, and although it would have been easy to stop myself, I didn't.

The kids emerged from the bathrooms to see me rolling away unattended. Olivia and Lily stood there, speechless, watching me go while Louise was oblivious to what was happening. There was no danger ahead of me, and the slight decline was carpeted, so I was not able to get up to an out-of-control speed. I wanted to see how far I would get and eventually stopped about twenty-five yards down the hallway. By the time I was slowing down, Louise had finished with the information desk and turned around to see me rolling away. The situation made us all laugh, and it lightened our somber, tired moods.

The last time I heard the girls laugh was when we were in the jeep bouncing around through the forests five days ago. Five days was too long to have pent-up anxiety without some laughter.

The drive home did not take long at all, as there was no traffic at two in the morning. At the beginning of the car ride, we all tried to make conversation, but it didn't last long as everyone was tired.

I enjoyed the quiet hum of snow tires on the asphalt highway as I looked out at the familiar landmarks approaching our home. Seeing the Ontario license plates on the surrounding cars, the roads that I knew, and the buildings that I had seen hundreds of times helped me relax, knowing that we were almost home and finally out of danger.

During the ride home, I did not mention our local hospital as I was hoping to arrive home and ignore the fact that they were waiting for me. Eventually, I know I will face the inevitable.

As we enter Brantford, I can smell the local bakery as the aroma of sugary icing enters the car. Not a bad aroma at all, as the surrounding countryside outside of Brantford, is all farms with just barren fields. But had it been spring or fall, the aromas could be completely different than sugar, cake, and icing.

We headed into our driveway: home. Getting out of the car, the air was cold, and patches of ice lined the driveway. It had not snowed for a while, and daytime temperatures could get above freezing. Our footsteps crunched up the driveway as we carried our luggage into our dark home.

It was unusual not to have our dog waiting for us, and I missed seeing her excitement. The family separated to their own rooms to drop their bags and get ready to sleep in their own comfortable beds. I went into the bathroom, and I stood looking at myself in the mirror, at my darkened eyes and swollen and bruised arms. I knew I was expected at the hospital. I did not want to leave. The last thing I wanted was to spend more time at a hospital. It was a horrible moment. I felt the comfort of my home, and I knew I had to leave, on my own accord, to admit myself to a hospital.

Louise was going to drive me there and make sure I was admitted then, return home to be with them and to get some much-needed sleep.

Louise knocked on the bathroom door and asked if I was ok. "Not really. I don't want to go back to a hospital," I replied through the door. Every part of me wanted to stay and collapse in my own bed. I felt physically and mentally exhausted. Ever since being sent back from God's presence, I have been feeling fine. I had actually been feeling great, having lost seven pounds from when I entered the Moron Hospital. Yes, I had been on medication, that could have been part of me not having any more heart palpitations or episodes of arrhythmia. I felt that I could at least spend the night and the next few hours at home.

Louise, very blunt and motherly, said through the door, "You don't have a choice. You have to go. They are waiting for you. I understand you not wanting to go, but you have to go and be checked."

I opened the door of the bathroom, took a look around the house, and was comforted by the warmth of being inside on an early February morning. I said, "Ok, let's go and get this over with."

Wednesday, at 3 a.m., Another Hospital

It's a short drive, less than five minutes from our home to the hospital, Brantford General. The short distance did not allow me much time to reflect on the decision to go to the hospital, which was a good thing, as it would make arriving there much more difficult. Thankfully, my experience with emergency rooms was minimal. I was tired, upset, and feeling emotionally drained when we arrived at the hospital. I had enough of nurses poking me with needles, making my arm swollen, and not truly caring. I wanted to be at home, tucked under my covers in my own bed.

Louise dropped me off at the entrance to the emergency room while she found parking. It was now 3:00 a.m., and thankfully, only about ten people were waiting. Every eye in that room shot toward me as I walked through the doorway. I suspected they were wondering why I was here and probably tried to diagnose me, to figure out if I was critical enough to jump ahead of them in the cue. Having walked into the room without assistance or a limp or blood streaming down, making a mess on the floor, I assume I am not a waiting room threat. The other potential patients dropped their heads back down and ignored me.

As I sat waiting for acknowledgment, I thought to myself that this waiting room did not look too bad and that I might only need to wait an hour or two to be seen. A nurse sat down opposite the glass barrier and asked for my national Health Card. Handing it through the little slot in the glass, she took it and checked it for a few seconds. "Oh, Mr. Robbins," she said as every eye in that waiting room rose to look at me. "We have been waiting for you. Please come right in," pointing towards the door leading to the small room she was in. As I rose up out of the chair looked around the room, everyone was looking at me. I felt empathetic towards them as I had been the one waiting and counting the number of people before me.

While the nurse checked my vitals, she asked about what had happened. I was only able to cover the basics of my experience: the palpitations, passing out, my heart rate, and the amount of time in the ICU. I handed over the medical records given to me by the Cuban Hospital Administration. "Here, this is what they gave me and told me to hand it to my doctor when I arrived home." I was told to go straight to the admissions area down the hallway. By the time I arrived at admissions, Louise was by my side. She had waited with me for only a few minutes before I was called for a medical ID bracelet.

After a few more minutes, an emergency nurse came through some swinging doors and called my name, "Mr. Robbins, please come in. We have been waiting for you!"

I had to say goodbye to Louise, and she said she was going to head home and pack some things for me. I was taken to the ER and given a bed where I was told to wait and the doctor would be in to see me shortly. A young and very fit nurse with shoulder-length blond hair pulled back came to my bedside,

"Hi, I'm Jen, Dr. Ajayi's head nurse in the ER," she said. "I heard you had some problems in Cuba!"

"Yeah, you could say that," I replied.

"Well, the first thing I need to do is establish an IV."

"You gotta be kidding me." I said, "Have a look at my arms; they stuck me more than eleven times, and my arms are swollen."

She looked at my arms and admitted that they looked pretty bad. Rhetorically, she asked, "Did they really know what they were doing?"

"From my recent experience, the doctors seemed to know a lot, but the nursing staff were more like glorified personal support workers."

After seeing my arms and the condition they were in, Jen displayed compassion, and her voice became gentle. From a professional perspective, she saw firsthand the aftermath of what I had been put through. I knew that my care in the Cuban ICU was substandard, but I just needed to deal with it as best I could. It was the only care that I could get, and I was in no position to complain or start making demands. Having Jen acknowledge what I suspected was difficult for me to hear, but I appreciated her compassionate demeanor. My frustration of having to get stuck by another needle was not driven by my phobia of needles, and it was that I had suffered trauma at the hands of my caregivers.

There are very few areas left on my arms that are suitable for an IV. With a calming voice, Jen explains why she needs to establish an IV, "I'm sorry, but I have to establish an IV. It is protocol in case anything were to happen with your health, and we need it to be ready just in case."

"Not having a choice is something that I seem to be getting used to." Knowing that both she and I do not have a choice, I said, "Well, I'm sure you have done this before."

Jen replied, "I'm pretty good. I will be gentle and try to get it on the first time."

Jen left to get the IV ready, and I felt my heart sink. I thought to myself, *here we go again. I just got out of the hospital nightmare, and here I am, back into the thick of it for round number two. At least I was back close to home. My family and everyone spoke English.*

While Jen was gone, I said a prayer. "Heavenly Father, you know I don't like needles, and I have been through so much. Please guide Jen with the IV and let her get it on the first try. Amen!"

Jen came back in just a couple of minutes later and looked over my two arms again. Both were badly bruised, but my left arm was much less swollen. I had hardly felt a thing when Jen exclaimed, "All done!" It was perfect on the first try. I felt relief and thankfulness for Jen's skill. It helped me to establish confidence regarding my future care and recovery in the hospital.

Shortly after Jen left, another nurse wheeled in a cart of vials and syringes. She was an older, more mature nurse and had a young woman following her. She introduced herself and said that they would need a blood sample for testing. The young lady was a student nurse for observation.

My worst nightmare was not ending! I said, "You have got to be kidding me! I have gone through this so much!"

She took one look at my arms and said, "Oh my, looks like you have gone through a lot. I'm not sure we will be able to find a good vein in those arms of yours."

She took my arms in her hand and examined them further. "Nope," she said, "Looks like we will have to draw a sample from a small vein in your hand. Is that okay with you? They generally hurt a little more."

I said, "If it is the only option, then you might as well go for it. Just promise me you are good and going to get it on the first try."

"I'm very good at this," she promised. "I have been doing it a long time. I'm actually training this young lady beside me. Being able to get a draw from a small vein will be a great training opportunity for us."

Reluctantly, I reply, "Well, I have been stuck so many times in the past few days. What's one more? I should be getting used to this by now anyway!"

She was gentle, and the vein on top of my hand was an easy target. Drawing the blood took longer than I was used to, as the vein was much smaller. It stung more, but the nurse was good and made conversation with me until it was over.

As I waited, I could see a doctor in the nurse's station. The nurses gathered around him as they looked at charts, files, and X-rays. They were discussing the contents of my brown file folder, and many of the nurses periodically looked at me. After much discussion amongst themselves, Dr. Ajayi made his way over to my bedside. I had been anticipating meeting Doctor Ajayi as he knew a little about what had happened to me in Cuba.

I knew he had a Christian faith, which was a comfort to me when the time came to explain my survival and what had actually happened.

"Hello, Mr. Robbins, I'm Dr. Abayomi Ajayi, but you can just call me Yomi. It is very nice to finally meet you. I have been trying to follow what has been going on with you from correspondence with my daughter and Olivia."

He is a gentle and nurturing man, and his bedside manner is comforting. Although he has a kind voice, his words were strong with knowledge and experience.

Yomi asked me about my experience in Cuba and what led up to being hospitalized. Yomi, after carefully listening to me, takes on a serious demeanor with deep concern in his voice.

"You are a very lucky man," he pointed up towards the ceiling and beyond. "Someone wants you here, has something more for you to do. You still have a purpose here on Earth. He wants you here for a reason, and I say that because, looking at your medical records and your ECG when you arrived at the hospital if you were my patient, I would have given you a ZERO percent chance of living. What happened to you was very serious, and there is no medical explanation for why you are still alive. Someone is looking out for you upstairs. Someone likes you and wants you here!"

I said to Yomi, "I know it was serious, and I know I didn't make it. I was sent back." Not surprised, because of his faith, he smiled, knowing that I was being truthful as it was the only explanation for me being alive. He didn't ask questions about my response but nodded in acceptance of what I confided.

Yomi continued, "We are going to keep you for a few days. We are sending you to the Hamilton General Hospital, which has a great cardiac unit. You will go there later today for an angiogram to rule out any blockage to the heart."

Yomi then told me to rest and, with a smile, said, "You are in good hands, and we will take care of you."

I said, "Thank you, and I appreciate everything."

Yomi left my little draped-in area. I continued to sit on the side of the bed while I took in everything he had said to me. A wave of emotion came over me, and I silently cried for the first time. With Dr. Ajayi's confirmation, tears ran down my cheeks, and I felt a huge emotional weight lift from me. Someone other than my immediate family knows I had a miracle. I had validation, and I can speak openly about the miracle. A physician believed me, and my medical documentation was confirmed.

My tears of relief became tears of gratitude towards God. Floodgates of thankfulness for God's mercy opened from within.

I had for so long held this wonderful power of my miracle pent up inside. I wanted to tell everyone about it. The situation in Cuba where secrecy caused me to be silent about my miracle. The Cuban doctors and nurses were not telling the truth to my family, my insurance, or my Embassy. I couldn't tell them that I knew I had died and that I knew I shouldn't be alive.

My mouth was being shut. The Holy Spirit was telling me to be quiet; otherwise, I could not have kept my mouth shut for so long. Usually, my life is an open book.

By the time Yomi returned to my bedside, I had composed myself, dried the tears from my cheeks, and steadied my breathing.

He informed me of my medical options, "I was able to pull some strings and call in some favors with colleagues. You have an angiogram scheduled for later today at the cardiac unit in Hamilton General Hospital. We will take you by ambulance. After your angiogram, you will not be staying in Hamilton General as they do not have any room for you there. You will be returning here by ambulance and admitted upstairs in one of our rooms." He continued, “You only have two options for treatment of your arrhythmia.”

I was listening intently as I did not want to miss anything in order to discuss my options with Louise when I saw her next. She would want answers, and I wanted to be able to explain everything to her without being ambiguous or open to negative interpretations and questions.

“First,” he continued, “you have the option to have an ICD, Implanted Cardio Defibrillator. It is a small box, battery, and computer like a pacemaker.”

I was a little shocked to hear the word “pacemaker” as my ninety-three-year-old great aunt, who had just passed away a couple of months earlier, had one for years, and it gave her limitations on activity levels and exposure to cold weather. Aware of the shocked look on my face when I heard “pacemaker,” Dr. Ajayi quickly continued, “An ICD is not a pacemaker. It only gets used when needed. If your heart goes into an arrhythmic state, it will give your heart an electric shock to reset its rhythm. It is like having your own personal IED defibrillator.”

I nodded my head in understanding but did not really like the idea of having something implanted in my chest. Dr. Ajayi could see my disappointment as there were not many options, and the only real fix was this surgery. Dr. Ajayi, knowing that I had two daughters and two daughters of his own, similar ages, gave his heartfelt opinion to me from one father to another.

He said to me in a calm and concerned tone, “It is a piece of security. Peace of mind every day. We don’t know what caused this to happen, and we don’t know if or when it will happen again. I can assure you that if this were to happen again without treatment, you would die. Do you want to live your life every day worrying if it will happen again? You have a young family that needs you and wants to be with you. The ICD is the only option to have assurance that every day you will be there for your family."

Again, in deep thought about what he had just told me, I nodded in understanding and acceptance of his words. I guess it is my only real option for a somewhat normal life with my family. Another surgery, more tests, more needles and tubes entering my body, more time away from home and my family, I was frustrated! My frustration was amplified by the fact that all this happened while we were on vacation. Vacations didn't come very often in my family, and I was having a difficult time coping with the timing of this.

I looked towards Dr. Ajayi for some insight into the timing of my medical emergency. In a somber tone, I rhetorically ask, "Why in Cuba, why on our vacation and why not here?"

In response to my tone of frustration, Dr. Ajayi took some time to think and then responded to me, "It was about timing, God's timing, and God's involvement as well. Many people have died from arrhythmia because they were alone…driving down a country road at night and ending up in a ditch, a person reading a book on a park bench alone, you were at least with people around you and close to a hospital. If you were alone or surrounded by people who didn't know you or care about you, you wouldn't have gotten the attention and care you needed. The doctors in Cuba are good, and you were able to get to the hospital." He continued, "I think the timing was good for you! Yes, you were on vacation, but you are here, and you are alive."

"For there is a time and a way for everything, although man's trouble lies heavy on him."

Ecclesiastes 8:6.

Dr. Ajayi continued, "I will come to you in your room after you get back from the angiogram at the other hospital. My head ER nurse, Jen, will be traveling with you to Hamilton General. Get some rest because you have had a long day."

Wednesday Morning, Lights Flashing and Siren Blasting

Louise returned to the hospital after packing some essentials for me. She brought a change of clothes, a toothbrush, toothpaste, a cell phone, a book, a pen and paper. I changed into clean clothing with her help, and although I didn't want her to leave, I was so tired and needed to try and sleep before my trip for the angiogram. Louise was also very tired and did not want to be away too long from the kids. The final night in Cuba, we had not slept well, and we are now going on 20 hours of wakefulness. I told Louise my two options. First was to do nothing, stay on medication, and hope for the best so that my heart does not go into arrhythmia again. If I did have my heart go into arrhythmia, I would, again, die. The second is to have heart surgery, where they would implant the ICD, giving me peace of mind that I would always be carrying backup security with me.

Louise said, "I guess it's only really one option! Sounds like the ICD is the only real option. You don't want to go through life worrying about when it will happen next, and the kids and I don't want to be constantly worried about if you are going to die one day. We as a family can't handle that!"

I replied, "I know and agree, but it sucks to have to go through with all this. It's the right thing to do, though. I can't go through life everyday thinking, is this the day my life is going to end? My wife loses her husband, and my kids their father."

The reality of my situation hit hard, and I knew my only real option was the ICD. Louise and I said, "Goodbye," but before she left, she advised me she would see me at the Hamilton Hospital later. After she left, I laid down on the bed and immediately went into a deep sleep.

I was not sure how long I slept or what time it was when Jen woke me and said my ambulance transfer was there waiting for us.

Jen grabbed my medical file, I took my personal belongings, and we were off towards the Ambulance Emergency door.

A paramedic was waiting for us with a rolling emergency bed. I was instructed to get on the bed. They strapped me in and wheeled me out to the waiting ambulance. I was wrapped in blankets, but the cold and damp February pinches my face. The inside of the ambulance is bright, and unlike the Cuban ambulance, this one was filled with life monitoring and saving equipment.

Jen hooked me to a heart rate monitor and took my vital information, which she then wrote in her notes. "All is good!" The friendly paramedics were busy getting everything ready for my transfer when Jen turned to the paramedic riding in the back of the ambulance with us and said to him, "Here, look at this." Like a parent boasting with pride over a child's gold star test results. Jen handed him my medical file and my ECG read-out from Cuba. The paramedic looked at the readout of my heart and said, "WOW!"

Jen said, "Have you ever seen anything like that?"

The paramedic, looking surprised and a little shocked, pointed towards me and asked, "Is this that guy?"

Jen said with a smile, "Yup!"

The paramedic responded, "You're still alive! I have never seen anything like that. That's crazy!" I can honestly say I did start to feel a little special.

The other paramedic sitting in the driver's seat turned towards us in the back and asked what kind of transfer it was, "Lights or no lights?"

Jen said, "Well, it is a V-TAC (ventricular tachycardia), so that justifies lights."

The driver excitedly said, "Right on!" and pulled away with the lights flashing and siren blasting, speeding towards the other hospital. At the speed we were going, the cardiac unit at Hamilton General was only about twenty-five minutes.

Jen, still looking over the records, said to me, "I can't believe you're alive. From these records, you shouldn't have made it."

I turned to Jen and asked, "Do you have faith?"

She stopped what she was doing, and I could tell she was thinking about the question. It took her a little time to answer, and she said, "Yes, I believe in something. I believe there is more to life, but I'm just not sure what."

I then said, "I didn't make it."

"What do you mean?" she asked.

"I didn't make it, I died, I was given a choice to come back or not, and I did to be with my daughters. Your charts are right. I didn't make it. I was with God, and He spoke to me and gave me a choice of which way to go, and I chose to come back."

Jen's response was sincere, "Wow, I have heard about that before around the hospital but never really took it that seriously."

I continued, "There is life after death. I never lost consciousness through the whole thing. I met God, who was light, and here I am!"

"I definitely need to think about that stuff because I have heard about that happening so many times before."

The rest of the ride to the hospital was quiet between us as she continued to monitor my vitals and occasionally grab something to hold onto to steady herself from the bumpy city streets. I feel good about finally telling someone other than my immediate family and Dr. Ajayi. I don't know if I made a difference in her life, but I am happy I planted a seed for thought that perhaps will make a difference to her later in life.

Once we arrived at the hospital, I was transferred to the care of the nurses in the cardiac unit. The nurses greet me by saying, "So you're the one from Cuba!" I smiled and said, "Yup, I guess that's me." The greeting made me feel important. This moment of feeling important was fleeting. Once in the cardiac ward, I was given my own private room and bathroom. I changed into a hospital gown, hooked up to an IV, and waited.

A nurse came into the room and started to explain the angiogram procedure. The people waiting outside of my room, in makeshift cubicles of drawn curtains, left one by one for their procedures. I knew I was going to be last as I was a last-minute addition to the already full roster of patients. And I waited and waited.

It was not until close to 7:00 pm that the nurse finally arrived to take me into the angiogram room. Upon entering, there were four people waiting and ready. I was placed on a cold stainless-steel table facing a large monitor that showed me an X-ray view. There was upbeat music playing, and everyone seemed to be very relaxed, which, in turn, made me feel more comfortable. Another IV was inserted into my wrist, this time in an artery.

A colored dye was injected through my artery, which traveled up my arm and across my chest to my heart. I could feel the dye traveling through. As soon as it hit my heart, I could feel incredible warmth through my head. It felt as though it was coming out of my ears. The results were immediate and showed that I did not have any blockages to or from my heart.

I was sent back to my room with a plastic clamp sealing the incision of my artery. Over the next hour, the nurse had to slowly release the pressure on the clamp until it could be completely removed. There was no room for me to stay at this hospital, so I waited until an ambulance transfer came to take me back to Brantford General Hospital. It was going to be close to twelve in the morning on Thursday before the ambulance was scheduled to arrive. I had another three hours of waiting ahead of me.

I had not had anything to eat since the plane ride back from Cuba the previous day. I was starving! I called Louise, and she agreed to come to Hamilton and wait with me. I asked her to bring food. She asked me what she should bring, and without any hesitation, I said pizza!

There was a pause and silence on her end of the phone. Louise then asked, "Are you sure you should be eating that? You are in a cardiac unit right now!"

I was so focused on my hunger that I had forgotten to tell her that my arteries were all clear.

"I'm good. There are no blockages in my arteries, and I can eat whatever I like. Besides, there are no other patients in the unit anymore. I'm the only one left, and nobody will see me eating pizza."

Louise reluctantly agreed to stop and get a slice of heaven for me and insisted I have a salad to go with it. Forty-five minutes had passed when Louise arrived with the slice of beloved pizza and a salad. I was so happy! A nurse soon came into my room, and I immediately went into defensive mode and said, "My arteries were all clear, so I thought this would be okay. Besides, I have been eating hospital food all week."

She smiled and gave a little nod, checked my dress, and then informed me that it was going to be at least another hour and a half before my transfer was to arrive.

It didn't matter. The pizza was awesome!

The room was darkened when I arrived as it was so late, and the other two patients in the room were already asleep. It was Wednesday night, and except for a couple of hours of sleep in the Emergency, I had been up for almost 48 hours, running mostly on adrenaline, a slice of pizza and salad. I was introduced to the night nurse, who was quite pleasant. She did some vital checks, had medication for me, and made sure I was comfortable. She said the doctor would see me the next day and wished me a good night.

It was close to 1 a.m. in the morning, and with my lack of sleep and exhaustion, I fell asleep quickly.

Thursday Morning, The Cuban Miracle

The light of day came too early for my liking. My room was on the fifth floor and had large bright windows that looked towards the north of the city, towards my home only five minutes away. It was comforting to see a familiar outside world. I had two roommates, Ron, who was in his mid-sixties, and an older, small-statured, sweet Italian lady named Moranna. Ron was the first to belt out, "Good morning, looks like we got a new roommate last night!" speaking to Moranna. Moranna looked towards me from across the room and waved with a nice smile. Ron was on the other side of the curtain divider, so I only heard his deep, loud voice filling the room. He moved the curtain to look at me. Ron was rough around the edges. He appeared to be a hard worker, perhaps in a skilled trade. He was a straight shooter, opinionated, and every so often throws humor into the conversation.

We each shared our stories without going into too much detail. Ron was in the hospital because of chest pains. He previously had bypass surgery and has had stints in his arteries. Moranna, who has a thick Italian accent, had experienced light headedness and felt her heart was weakening. Both were scheduled for the same angiogram procedure that I just finished. It was Thursday, and they were not scheduled for the procedure until Friday. The same day, I'm going to have the ICD implant.

Breakfast was to be served soon, and I was really looking forward to having something to eat. When breakfast finally arrived, I peeled off the lids with enthusiasm. My excitement turns to wonder. Not the good wonder but rather the wonder of what the heck I was about to eat! The nursing care I endured in Cuba compared to the quality of nursing back home in Canada was like night and day. The food was the complete opposite.

Louise called my cell that morning and asked if I needed anything. I said, "Something to eat because I cannot eat what they brought me and a decaf coffee."

Louise then asked if any of my roommates wanted anything. Moranna declined, but Ron asked for a coffee, double-double, and was appreciative for the offer. Louise then commented that our new pastor, Lance, was going to stop by later today for a visit. This is great news for me as I really feel the need to tell more people about my time with God, and he would be someone who would understand and fully appreciate my story.

Louise's visit was fantastic. Not only did I eat a satisfying sandwich and coffee, but it was great being able to socialize with her in a more relaxed manner than in Cuba. Although still in a hospital setting, I felt safe and less of a need to choose my words carefully. After Louise's visit, I was able to relax, rest, read, and walk the halls of the fifth floor of the hospital.

I was also able to take my first stand-up shower in seven days.

Dr. Ajayi came in for a follow-up in the afternoon. He advised me about the angiogram. All my arteries were clear. He then talked about the events that I had to look forward to the next day regarding the heart surgery implanting the ICD. I was to leave in the late morning for Hamilton General Hospital. I would arrive at the cardiac unit to have the ICD implant procedure, which takes an hour to an hour and a half. Then, I will be transferred back to Brantford General for the night, hopefully, I will be home by Saturday afternoon. Sounded great to me! I have a plan laid out for me and anticipate being home with my family.

Thursday evening, Pastor Lance poked his head through the door and came into the room with a welcoming smile. I was extremely happy to see him and very eager to tell him my story. I have not known Lance for very long. I have gone to the church for a couple of years, but only on certain occasions like Christmas and Easter, with a couple more visits in between. Lance was a youthful and dynamic speaker. He had the ability to address everyday needs.

I was excited to share my story with someone new, and the relief was Lance absorbed every word of my testimony. He listened without interruption, with total acceptance and a sincere "Wow" by the time I finished. My Father used to visit people in the hospital, share the Bible with them, and pray with them. I'm thankful he was able to do that for people. I now understand how it feels to have someone care about you and be candid about God in conversation. Pastor Lance, before leaving, prayed with me and for me.

Immediately after Lance had left the room, Ron spoke up from behind the curtain between us.

"Was that your Minister?" he asked.

I replied, "Yes, it was."

"Seemed like a nice fellow. Nice of him to come here and visit you!"

"It's a new church for me. I just started going more regularly not long ago, and yes, the pastor was a nice person, nice enough to come by and visit."

Silence stretched for a short period of time between the curtain.

Ron then asked, "Was that true, what you told the pastor?"

I said, "Yes, it was as real as I am lying here in this room."

"Well, I never really believed in that kind of stuff," Ron said. He continued, "I know there's something, but I never really thought about it that much."

It was new to me not to feel shy or nervous talking about my near-death experience. It was the truth, and I experienced it first-hand. I lived it, felt it, and I knew the absolute truth about the existence of life after death. There was no wavering in my belief, and I could speak about it with certainty.

I replied, "You should think about it. What happened to me was real. Your life doesn't end after you die. If I were you, I would take the time to know what will happen to you once you die. Your life continues. I never lost consciousness once, not even for a second, and I was fully aware of what was happening."

"Well," he said, "That's a pretty great story, and you don't seem like the type of person to make that kind of stuff up. I guess I should think about it because we're not here forever."

Not a pushy or preachy person, I left the conversation alone. I felt like I had said enough to stir his interest and perhaps plant a seed of faith in his mind. If Ron wanted to ask more questions, I was there to try and answer him. I felt good about Ron questioning my story, and I could tell he was honestly intrigued.

Today is the day for surgery, back at the Hamilton Hospital. Ron and Moranna were both going to the same hospital for their angiogram. She seemed nervous. Ron and I were as comforting as we could be with her. We told her not to worry, the procedure was easy and nothing to worry about. We stated that it was quick and painless and that she would do great. I know we made her feel better, but she was still terribly nervous.

Ron was the first to leave, and after he left, I could still see the worry on Moranna's face. It was just Moranna and I in the room, and I felt empathy for her.

I ask from across the room, "Would you like me to pray with you?"

She slowly nodded her head and said in her thick Italian accent, "Yes, that would be nice."

I sit on the edge of her bed. Her hand reached out towards mine. Holding her hand in mine, we prayed for a safe procedure and for God to be with her and the doctors as well and to comfort her.

In a soft, more relaxed tone, Moranna sincerely said, "Thank you."

I left for Hamilton General Hospital at noon. Once there, I was taken to the ICD operating clinic and admitted. As I was being transferred from the ambulance to the operating clinic, the nurse escorting us started to read my chart. A surprised look came across her face as she looked towards me and proclaimed, "Oh, so you're the Cuban miracle!"

I laughed a little and said, "Yup. That's me."

"Well," she said, "Pretty amazing that you are here with us."

It's nice to have recognition, but I wish it were for some other type of accomplishment!

Louise came to the hospital with me for the long wait. Although I experienced a long wait in pre-op, I was grateful, having accepted my fate, to be getting it done and move on with my life and attempt to get back to some normalcy.

Now, after having two days to relax and decompress, I have a better understanding and more of an acceptance of my near-death experience. Looking back, I felt like my experience was cut too short. I didn't see loved ones waiting for me. Although I felt their presence, I did not get to meet God or Jesus and have a meaningful conversation where I could ask pertinent questions about life and our human existence. I wished that I had stalled and bought some more time to look around. Perhaps a little longer, and I would have seen heaven and past loved ones. I thought, 'Well, next time if it ever happens again, I will be smarter about it and prolong my time there. I would force myself to look around, ask more questions, and stay longer in that incredible love.' I took this thought to the operating room. I was, in a way, hoping for another chance to visit the heavenly realm.

Entering the operating room, I did not have any fear. Either way, good or bad, I knew I was going to be ok.

The operating room was sterile and cold. I was transferred onto a stainless-steel table and looked around the room. I saw mostly stainless-steel mechanicals and a lot of large bright lights. The people in the operating room were friendly, and they said I would feel some pressure and prodding around my chest. As they were talking, the room began to echo, time seemed to slow, and the room became surreal, like in a Salvador Dali painting. The voices in the room started to meld together and developed into a low-tone mumble. I was out!

Louise was waiting for me when I recovered. I had a large compression bandage over my left chest. Although it was not hard to breathe, it felt like someone was standing on my chest. I was told by the nurse that everything went very well, and I was going to be transferred back to my local Brantford hospital for the night to finish my recovery there. I was happy that the operation went well and that I was one step closer to being home and seeing my kids again.

There was also a small part of me wishing that I had another near-death experience. I missed being there. I wanted to access that adventure again with the idea of being in good hands here on earth to bring me back to my family. When the ambulance transfer came to get me, Louise and I said our goodbyes as she left to return to the kids.

Friday Night, Home at Last

Arriving back in my room at Brantford General, I felt concerned about my comfort. I did not want to disturb my wound by rolling around in my sleep. I tried to get comfortable in my bed and sat up so as not to be able to comfortably roll over. Once a bit more relaxed and in a modestly comfortable position, it did not take long for me to fall fast asleep. As exhausted as I was, I did wake sometime in the early hours of a dark morning in uncomfortable pain. Apprehensively grabbing the nurse call button, I pushed down and waited at most a minute before a nurse arrived. I explained to her that there was enough discomfort under the bandage on my chest that I was finding it very difficult to sleep. The nurse came back with something for my pain. Quite quickly, my pain had subsided, and I drifted off into a deep sleep.

The next morning, Ron and Moranna were both awake before me. We all said our good mornings, and then Ron, unable to contain himself and with a bit of laughter, said, "Well, you won that round of snoring last night. I thought I was bad the night before, but you definitely succeeded in getting me back last night! I guess it was a bit of revenge."

I laughed and apologized. "Yeah, I can get going pretty good. I was really tired and haven't had much sleep the past few days."

As I finished apologizing, I looked over towards Moranna, and she had a very concerned look on her face as she looked back towards me. Shaking her head at me, she said in her thick accent, "That is no good! That is no good for you like that!" I couldn't decipher whether she was truly concerned or angry. I think it was a bit of both concern for my health and anger that I had perhaps woken her.

Again, I apologized and said that I should get it looked at.

"It's no good like that. You need to see something about that!"

Ron agreed with her and said the walls and windows were shaking. I had obviously won the competition with Ron, and taking this win, I was very happy for both Ron and Moranna that I was expected to go home later that day.

Breakfast came to the room, and I did not really know what it was, so I did not eat it. Louise called me on my cell phone and asked if she could bring anything. I asked for breakfast and a decaf coffee. Ron asked for a large coffee. About thirty minutes had passed when Louise arrived, and I was able to eat. I asked about our daughters, and Louise said that they were doing well. Olivia and Lily were slowly adjusting back to life at home. They had stayed home from school, and Louise informed their teachers and principals about what had happened. They needed some time before heading back to school. Counseling was offered, but the kids felt they just needed some time. They didn't want to go back to their peers and be bombarded with questions about their vacation and forced to relive the experience through their words. They didn't know how to talk about it or how to explain what had happened. They didn't want to try to explain what had happened. Kids in their classrooms came from many different religious backgrounds, some with beliefs separate from ours and many without any faith. My girls knew any discussion would necessitate expressing that God was the one who saved me, not the medical experts. They wouldn't have to get into all the details of what happened, but if the questions led them to God being the answer, they were not ready to continue that conversation due to possible marginalization.

After a short morning visit, Louise left to go back with the girls, and I knew it would not be long before I was home again. It was about 3:00 pm when I was finally discharged from the hospital and was advised my recovery would be at home and a follow-up with a cardiologist.

Saturday Afternoon, I finally arrived at home.

I was greeted by Olivia, Lily, and our big, hairy, beautiful dog, Shiloh. The familiarity and warmth of our home were comforting after my stressful absence. Shiloh sensed something about me was different, and her greeting was subdued. After a few pats on her head and some loving scratches, she was done and resumed her position on her bed.

Olivia and Lily were interested in how I was doing, and we talked about what had happened over the past few days of being separated. Trying to get comfortable to rest and sleep was very difficult. The pressure from the bandage and the swelling on my chest was very restrictive with positions of comfort. Our black leather recliner chair in our finished basement was my best bet for finding a comfortable position. While in my back leather recliner, the rest of the family left me alone for many hours in order for me to rest and recover. I rested and slept as much as I could.

There was a lot of time for me to be able to relax in solitude, think about what we had just gone through, and ponder further my time in the presence of God.

7 Whither shall I go from thy spirit? Or whither shall I flee from thy presence?

8 If I ascend up into heaven, thou art there: if I make my bed in hell, behold, thou art there.

9 If I take the wings of the morning and dwell in the uttermost parts of the sea;

10 Even there shall thy hand lead me, and thy right hand shall hold me.

Psalm 139: 7-10 KJV

Epilogue

This book is about truth, my truth, both good and bad. I have not told this part of my experience to very many people prior to writing this book. It is personal and intimidating. I'm not going to go into too much detail, but I do feel it needs to be told.

The "Veil" is very thin between this world we live in and God's heavenly realm, and there are evil forces against us! Right now, I'm sitting back in my office chair at one thirty in the morning, contemplating how to continue with these events that happened. I do not want to be an alarmist, but it is part of my story. I don't want to frighten anyone, as it is not the purpose of my story. My story is about truth, love, and compassion, which God has for all. Knowing life continues after our earthly death should be comforting, and that is my purpose in writing my story.

Essentially, I died twice in one day.

The first time was in the jeep, as we entered the city limits of Moron, while the second was in the Hospital General De Moron.

After I pulled over in the jeep, took the car out of gear, and pressed the emergency flashers, blackness clouded my vision, my children's voices became a distant echo, and there was nothing but blackness. It was as if I had just fainted or blacked out. I had no near-death experience despite witnesses reporting I had stopped breathing. My skin went purple and blue from lack of oxygen, and my blood pressure dropped either so low or completely that my skin caved in. I was in this state for approximately a minute and saw nothing except blackness, and I had no sense of consciousness.

I feel I was not in the right place or at the right time. I should have stayed dead. My heart had obviously stopped functioning, and there was no resuscitation to counter or correct my condition. Miraculously and against medical reasoning, I stayed alive for at least the next hour and a half until I was in the hospital and physically separated from my children. God kept me alive until a couple of minutes after they left the room. I felt that they were the ones being protected that day. There was no other reason for me to survive that long, with a heart rate of over 220 beats per minute.

I laugh about this now when I think about how stubborn I was for not getting to a hospital sooner. I think about my guardian angel and how much effort and frustration it would have taken to keep me alive for so long. God had control and authority over the time it took for me to get to the hospital. He kept me alive for the benefit of my children, not seeing their dad perish in front of them. The hospital did not resuscitate either, so the only difference was that my children were not present. God kept me alive for the benefit of others. He could see the whole picture from every angle and understand the complexity of every situation.

The medical report stated cyanosis, where the body tissue turns a bluish-purple hue from lack of oxygen to the red blood cells. Immediately following, I went into convulsions from a seizure. Before the cyanosis and convulsions, I was already in my wonderful, peaceful soul space. I had no idea what was going on outside of where I was. My consciousness was in a peaceful sea of white. I did not feel anything internally or externally. I was completely shut off from the outside world. I inherently knew I was still in my body. My soul and physical body had not yet separated. My soul protected me from any physical pain or discomfort resulting from the outside world. My soul was still in my body but separated from its physicality until the timing was right for me to leave this world. This was my experience, so I cannot say that it would be the same for everyone. What I do know is that I was protected from pain and trauma before I was taken out of my body and before my physical death.

"The saying 'You can't take it with you!' is so absolutely true.

When you leave this life on earth, you are completely stripped down to nothing except your consciousness, your soul, and who you are, with respect to your personality and how you think. The earth fell away, and everything with it was gone. Accumulation of stuff doesn't matter and means nothing once you die. Your stuff can become someone else's burden on earth. There is nothing wrong with having nice things and a comfortable living. You can't take money with you, but you can take greed, selfishness, self-righteousness, pride and anger. For a period after I returned, I was not motivated to financially succeed. I became depressed and disenchanted, realizing how important money was to so many people where dishonesty and greed rule over love and compassion. My motivation to succeed became less about being superficially successful and more about becoming successful in order to help others.

A number of NDE experiencers have stated in testimonials that they felt "Home." Passing away from this dimension's life was like going home to where they felt they belonged. Although I did not have that realization in the midst of my NDE, upon reflection, I, too, must agree that the afterlife was a more natural and appropriate place to be. On earth, our souls are bound by matter. We are in human bodies that are mere vehicles to navigate this universe. Our bodies are heavy, burdened by gravity, constrained, and limiting us in abilities. After I died and separated from my body, I had an immense amount of freedom of movement and a sense of release from having been bound by mass and gravity. Imagine having inconsequential freedom to roam around naked, not being confined by constricting, sometimes heavy, uncomfortable clothing. Taking it one step further, an existence without the physical confines of a body. Weightlessness results in unobstructed movement by thought. Not having a body and existing only as a soul consciousness was very freeing. It did feel natural and proper. Being back on earth, although lovely, and I am in awe of God's creation every day, does not feel natural or normal to me anymore. I feel like an imposter and have a strengthened knowledge and understanding that this time on earth is only temporary and a very small part of our existence. We are in this world but not of this world!

When I got back from the hospital, Brantford General, and finally settled in at home recovering in my own bed, I was spiritually attacked twice in my dreams. During my near-death experience, I discovered the truth of life after death, God's existence, His love for us, and His authority over His creation. I was close to God and experienced his unrelenting love. I was in His love, and I felt He was in me. It was a close and personal experience with Him. Knowing and experiencing the truth made me a target. For Satan, I knew and experienced too much. Demons are evil! They were mad that I came back, and I knew the truth.

My dreams were very vivid and memorable. The first time I was attacked, my dream led me into an underground domed chamber. There were Egyptian-like hieroglyphic depictions covering the interior of the dome. There was a walkway around the interior of the dome, and in the center was hot lava and fire. As I entered the chamber and started to explore the inner edge, demonic entities appeared and started to torment me. The torment became physical and was sharp, stinging, cutting pain as they slashed at me. It was like my skin was being torn open. I tried fighting them off, but there were too many, and it was intensifying. The dream and the pain became too real, and I knew that this was not a normal nightmare. Not able to defend myself, I called out to Jesus, and within seconds, He descended as a being of white light and wearing a white robe. He floated towards the middle of the room, and with outreached arms, He filled the interior with intense white light. His light immediately engulfed and dispersed the demonic spirits. The intensity of the light-filled my vision, and I woke up.

I was startled, shaken, and wide awake in the comfort of my darkened bedroom. The dream was more intense and radically different than any other dream I had experienced. Jesus appeared immediately when I cried for help, and He demonstrated his power and authority over the demonic spirits. I prayed and thanked Jesus for His intervention and for helping me. I took a few minutes to settle myself, and eventually, I felt safe and was able to get back to sleep.

A few days passed and again, I was in the midst of a dream that became all too painfully real. There was one demon that caught my attention as a highly sexual being and drew me closer, only to strike out at me. I immediately recognized that this, again, was not right. Now, from my previous dream, knowing that Jesus has my back and that I am a creation of God and loved by God, I commanded an end to the torment. The entity left as I was determined to have the torment stop and then I woke up, again shaken, wide awake, and hyper-aware of my surroundings.

Having a near-death experience was both terrible and exhilarating. The events leading up to dying and the aftermath of hospitalization and recovery were mentally and physically difficult. The actual dying was easy, and the time spent out of my body and in God's presence was astonishingly beautiful. It was a positive experience filled with peace, no fear, and a love so powerful that it cannot be fully comprehended with respect to our earthly knowledge and understanding. I feel blessed to have had the opportunity to experience what is to come after this life on earth.

On many occasions, it has also been difficult to be back and have to deal with the realities of life on Earth. Many of the realities on earth, such as jobs, income, stress, fighting, depression, and physical pain, did not exist where I was, so having to deal with those aspects of life now is, for me, taking a step backward.

One of the more profound realizations and lessons I have received from this experience is about faith, acceptance, and knowing that God is not a distant hierarchy being on a throne somewhere, uninterested in our daily plight here on earth. In church, hearing over the years about the necessity of having a relationship with God and how He walks beside us in our lives is a difficult concept to accept and completely understand. I now know this to be true as I was looked after every step of my medical emergency, and there was purpose and timing to what had transpired. Bad things happen to good people, and to understand and accept this earthly reality, one needs to accept that there is a purpose to everything in life. God knows exactly what is happening in our daily lives and walks beside us every day.

The hands of time have continued to turn, and years have passed. Life is still a struggle. Similar to the struggles I had biking through the steep mountainous terrain, sweat, pain, and physical and mental fatigue carry on in many aspects of my earthly life. God, like the cheering race spectators, family members, fellow racers, and teammates, wants us to succeed and supports our efforts. God, and especially faith in God, is our support through the race of our lives. Life and our pursuit of happiness is the mountain we are climbing. Experiencing and knowing that God is with me and my family helps me accept the struggles and hardships. I know that He is present in my life. I have learned to trust in God with all things in my life, good and bad. I am acknowledged, recognized, and loved through all things. Knowing God's authority, when there is a struggle in my life or something tragic, I know that there is a purpose and reason behind everything, and I trust in God to get through.

My health may fail and my spirit may grow weak but God remains the strength of my heart; He is mine forever.

Psalm 73: 26

Printed in Great Britain
by Amazon

48047042R00116